ROBERT ADAM
1728–92
Architect of Genius

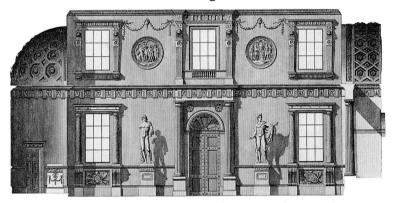

JULIUS BRYANT

English Heritage

NATIONAL LIBRARY of SCOTLAND

sponsored by

The London Historic House Museums Trust

The Ante-Room at Syon House, Brentford, Middlesex, the house remodelled by Robert Adam between 1761 and 1769. The use of the marble columns, in Adam's words, was intended 'to form the room and heighten the scenery'. The whole is typical of the 'Adam style' of interior decoration, known to millions today through country house visiting. (A.F. Kersting)

Contents

Supper at a fête-champêtre *in the Fête Pavilion, The Oaks, Carshalton, in June 1774, showing the 'art of living', for which Adam was designing, in full swing. Detail from an engraving in Robert and James Adam's* Works in Architecture *(by courtesy of the Trustees of Sir John Soane's Museum).*

Perspectives

Adam's Achievement

In the history of British architecture, few men have become not only a household name, but a part of the English language. 'Adam' is defined by the *Oxford Dictionary of Current English* as 'of the decorative style created by the brothers Robert and James Adam in the 18th century'. For much of the last century the word was used in the plural, but the lion's share of responsibility for creating the Adam style is now credited to Robert. One of the few British geniuses to have been recognized internationally in his own day, Robert Adam had an influence stretching from North America to Russia. According to his obituary in the *Gentlemen's Magazine* in 1792, 'Mr Adam produced a total change in the architecture of this country'.

Adam's achievement is all the more remarkable when we realize that he left no single masterpiece that might serve as a summary of his abilities. We have the Queen's House by Inigo Jones, Wren's St Paul's, Vanbrugh's Blenheim Place, Gibbs' St Martin-in-the-Fields, Burlington's Chiswick House and Chambers' Somerset House. But against Adam's name in this avenue of classic British buildings there is a conspicuous gap, and instead a winding path leading to a series of country houses, town houses and public buildings, few of which have escaped extensions, remodelling or demolition.

Nevertheless, the Adam style is instantly recognizable today, when the appetite for country house visiting seems keener than ever before. He created a unique synthesis of all the visual arts, uniting porticos and pedestals, columns and carpets in a single style that evokes the world of classical Greece and Rome, in a way peculiarly suited to the British temperament. Adam's picturesque classicism assures his continuous prominence in the British pantheon, alongside contemporaries such as Reynolds, Gainsborough, 'Capability' Brown and Chippendale.

In the 'story' of British architecture, Robert Adam dominates the third quarter of the eighteenth century. He eclipsed the fashionable followers of the sixteenth-century Venetian architect Andrea Palladio by asserting the creative liberty of the architect as artistic genius. In this, he claimed the authority of classical precedent, for he recognized the freedom from 'rules' enjoyed by the architects of ancient Rome, particularly in their domestic architecture. Adam challenged the academic conventions of the Anglo-Palladian movement, pointing to their derivation from temples and other forms of civic architecture. Building on the example of Lord Burlington's artist-architect William Kent (1685–1748), Robert Adam addressed every aspect of interior decoration. He enriched the available vocabulary of classically inspired ornament and brought to the planning of room sequences and to exterior design an artist's eye for 'picturesque' effects and a gentleman's knowledge of the continental 'art of living'.

Like Kent, Adam was a 'Renaissance Man', combining the gifts of an architect, businessman, painter, scholar, writer, antiquarian and designer of sculpture, metalwork, carpets and furniture. As a designer of buildings he ranged from castles to coffee houses, churches to urban planning schemes. His gift as a designer lay in an astonishing sense of scale, whether in the relative proportions of adjacent rooms, the vast prospects to be enjoyed from the windows of a country house saloon, or the quiet relationship between the decoration of a chair leg and a door knob.

Behind this versatility and prolific output lay a driving ambition, not for wealth, fame or artistic 'freedom' as such, but a worldly, competitive ambition to be the greatest architect of his great age. Ironically, his influence was such that the 'story' of British architecture in the eighteenth century concludes with the degeneration of the characteristic 'Adam style', largely through fashionable imitations, and a return to scholarly sources in the 'Greek Revival'.

Adam Today

Mention 'Adam' to a country house goer and the mind is soon awash with sphinxes, paterae, medallions, swags, fans, arabesques and anthemion motifs. The difficulty in appreciating Adam today lies in the very familiarity of his name and style, and the perceptions which can militate against any fresh response to his work. Like Chippendale and 'Capability' Brown his contribution is seen almost as the style of his age, rather than of his own distinguishable *oeuvre*.

The difficulty in understanding Adam also derives, ironically, from the sheer volume of writings on him. After a fall from favour in the nineteenth century, the Adam family's works have fed a swelling bibliography. A clear tradition in approach became established. Robert Adam's career is often divided into four phases: his early years in Scotland and his Grand Tour to Rome (1750–58); English country houses (1760s); London town houses (1770s), and public buildings, particularly in Edinburgh (1780s). This provides a basis for exploring the development of the 'Adam style' through buildings, even though several projects took over a decade to complete and overlap. Recently the importance of a fifth area of Adam's activities, his designs for castles, has been recognized.

One key to seeing Adam as he saw himself is provided by *The Works in Architecture*. First published by Robert and James Adam in parts from 1773 until 1779 (with a posthumous volume in 1822) this amounts to the brothers' personal manifesto and catalogue. The choice of subjects for the lavish engravings contrasts with the more familiar projects, particularly country houses, with which Adam's popularity is identified today. The text reveals preoccupations beyond artistic sources and stylistic development. Together with early correspondence and Robert Adam's publication *The Ruins of the Palace of the Emperor Diocletian at Spalatro* (1764), this provides a basis for introducing the 'Adam style' primarily in terms of Robert Adam himself, as artist, entrepreneur, gentleman of profession and man of thought.

'My notions of architecture'

Robert Adam's genius was that of an artist rather than of a theorist. The evolution of the Adam style was empirical, not based on fully worked out intellectual principles. As Robert told the Edinburgh judge and philosopher Lord Kames, he had 'but few moments to dedicate to theory and speculation' in 1763. His younger brother James is credited with authorship of the prefaces of the *Works*, and some of the text tallies, almost word for word, with an unpublished essay written by James in 1762. But we should not assume that theory simply followed designs, that Robert's understanding of planning, elevations and interior decoration was entirely instinctive, and that his preoccupation with the practical pressures of a business practice indicates any want of a theoretical mind.

Robert's thoughts on architecture are interwoven with his younger brother's literary aspirations as an architectural theorist. Whilst in Rome Robert planned a publication on the Baths of Diocletian and Caracalla, and before leaving to begin the *Spalatro* project in April 1757 he declared:

> my Baths are now all completed and to be sure it has cost me a deal of trouble and plague.

Now I must begin to write the description for it, being determined, in imitation of Scotch heroes, to become author, to attack Vitruvius, Palladio and those blackguards of ancient and modern architecture, sword in hand.

In his unpublished introduction to the *Ruins of . . . Spalatro*, written the same year, Robert Adam revealed once again his own intellectual response to architecture, one which he must have passed on to his younger brother on his return to Britain in 1758. Referring to the Roman Public Baths of Caracalla and Diocletian, Robert records:

> On them, therefore, I bent my particular attention and though any accident should for ever prevent me from publishing to the world my drawings and reflections on that subject yet I must own they contributed very much to the improvement of my taste and enlarged my notions of architecture.

In the absence of any unpublished architectural treatise written by Robert alone, the *Works* must provide the best introduction to the true principles of the 'Adam style'.

James Adam, painted by Allan Ramsay in 1754. Ramsay originally painted James holding a design in 'Gothick' taste, for which a Palladian plan was soon substituted, no doubt to establish the architect's credentials. (Laing Art Gallery, Newcastle upon Tyne / Tyne and Wear Museums)

The Age of Reason

Architecture, more than any other art form, is the product of its time through its dependence upon patronage, and Adam's achievements are inseparable from the political, economic and intellectual issues of his day.

Robert Adam's Scottish background provides several keys to his outlook and achievement. He was born in Kirkcaldy, on 3 July 1728. His father, William Adam, became the most eminent architect of his day in Scotland. But as a second son Robert could not expect to inherit his father's practice and main estate, Blair Adam. Following the Act of Union of 1707, which removed political control of 'North Britain' to Westminster, ambitious Scots before Adam had headed south to London where 16 Scottish peers and 45 MPs sat in Parliament. Scots also had strong links with Europe, particularly France and Rome, where the Jacobite supporters of the Stuart claim to the British crown lived in exile. The Scots' success in attaining political high office in England and the strength of Scottish expatriate support for their fellow countrymen were major factors in Adam's rise. The exact nature of Adam's own political motivations is still unresearched, but he served as MP for Kinross-shire from 1768 until 1774.

The accession of King George III in 1760 was followed by a period of relative peace when international commerce was able to prosper, aided by the 'Industrial Revolution'. In 1763 the completion of the Seven Years' War left Britain the victor in the colonial struggle with France over India and North America, securing new sources and markets. Rebellion in the American colonies from 1774 led to the defeat of the British forces in the

War of Independence (concluded in 1783) and a loss of interest in speculative investment. Architecture is some gauge of wealth, and 610 country houses were built between 1760 and 1800, even after the great building 'boom' of the British Palladian movement, which produced 230 houses between 1710 and 1759. Only three new great houses were begun between 1780 and 1800, a period of recession which clouded the last decade of Adam's career and life.

Patriotism and prosperity at the outset of the reign of the new monarch brought fresh hopes of an age of patronage akin to Renaissance Italy and to Rome under its first Emperor, Augustus. Britain's 'Augustan Age' believed the time had come for a native British school of artists and architecture to do justice to its sense of political and economic supremacy. The appropriate style was the architecture of ancient Greece and Rome.

Patriotism ran alongside an attitude which today might be termed 'Europeanism'. Peace facilitated travel on the Continent and artists and gentlemen completed their training with the 'Grand Tour' to Rome. An international community of artists and patrons grew up in Rome, creating new opportunities for artistic debate and stylistic exchange. A succession of lavish publications crossed national boundaries, competing to meet the demand for fresh evidence of the classical world, of a world that might be emulated and surpassed. Adam's *Spalatro* and *Works*, with their impressive lists of international subscribers, followed a series of publications, including Piranesi's *Antiquita Romane* (1748), Robert Wood's *Ruins of Palmyra* (1753), Wood and Dawkins's *Ruins of Baalbek* (1757), and Stuart and Revett's *Antiquities of Athens* (1762–89).

The notion of art and architecture as having a formative influence on the development of taste and, in turn, of a true 'gentleman' contributed to an ambivalence in the social status of artists. The rise of the professions is a theme of the era of direct relevance to Adam, who travelled in Europe as the younger son of a professional but with all the airs and graces of a British aristocrat. His driving ambition to achieve recognition as an architect and gentleman had its parallels in the career of Sir Joshua Reynolds and Sir William Chambers, respectively first President and Treasurer of the Royal Academy, the institution founded in 1768 to further the arts of painting, sculpture and architecture.

Robert Adam had a distinct advantage over many other professionals in enjoying an intellectual upbringing. While their future rivals had to rise through the lowly ranks of a profession then regarded as little different from that of a builder or mason, the Adam brothers enjoyed a liberal education, their home frequented by Edinburgh's great men of learning, their conversation free to share the themes of the Scottish Enlightenment. Some of the greatest Scottish philosophers and historians of the day were directly associated with Robert Adam's family, notably his cousin William Robertson, Adam Smith, Adam Ferguson, Alexander Carlyle and David Hume.

The period saw a fundamental belief in the ability of man to progress through academic study, industry and rational discourse, rivalled by a conviction of the genius of individuals, free to create from their own inspiration, according to aesthetic values such as the Sublime, Picturesque and Beautiful. The classical world of Greece and Rome seemed to provide a model of political and social culture which might even be surpassed in this age of achievement. This tension, between the legacy of the past and the creative freedom of the individual in the present, is a further issue which will arise when we explore Adam's ambitions and architecture.

Adam's Social Position

Robert Adam's own working career only began in earnest on his return from Rome in 1758. Until then, the first thirty years of his

Medallion of Robert Adam by James Tassie,
c.1792.

life bear little resemblance to the formative years of an aspiring artist. After a university education and then employment in the family practice he travelled on the Grand Tour in great style, initially in the company of the Hon. Charles Hope, younger brother of the Earl of Hopetoun. On his return Adam set up house in London, in St James's Place, and then in Lower Grosvenor Street, Mayfair. Ten years later he entered Parliament. His ventures, like his years in Italy, were backed financially by the family business. As a younger son of the most distinguished and successful Scottish architect, Robert Adam was, in effect, Scottish gentry. His older brother John inherited the Blair Adam estate and, although a laird, he retained responsibility for the family business, inheriting his father's position as Master Mason to the Board of Ordnance.

Robert faced the younger son's need to pursue his own career. The social divide between affluent professionals and the younger sons of the aristocracy was narrow and uncertain, and the question of Adam's 'place' in society as a working gentleman clearly underlay his motivations and relations with patrons. His exceptional background must have contributed to his rise to prominence, for Adam was in a position to share the values, fashionable taste and social graces of his young patrons. His Scottish birth, far from being a hindrance, was an essential ingredient in his success at finding patrons to launch his career in England. Alongside these factors the handsome architect's personal charm and business acumen undoubtedly played no small part in his success.

Foundations

The Family Business

Until he was eighteen Robert Adam aspired to be a painter, rather than an architect, but on leaving Edinburgh College (as the University was then known) in 1746 he joined his older brother John as an apprentice in their father's practice. Two years later their father died and John became head of the family, which numbered four brothers and six sisters.

The brothers continued their father's work at Fort George on the Moray Firth (the end of a line of forts along the Caledonian Canal erected as a consequence of the '45 Rebellion). They also managed his business as a wholesale supplier of materials for the building trade, with warehouses at Leith. In 1750 they received their first major commission, the interior of Hopetoun House near Edinburgh, which followed on from their father's remodelling and extension of the exterior in the 1740s. Five country houses were begun by John and Robert by October 1754, when Robert joined Lord Hopetoun's younger brother on his Grand Tour to Italy.

William Adam's intention had been that all his sons should receive the best possible training in architecture, and that included visiting the Continent. However, his death aged fifty-eight, and Robert's ambitions, meant that John chose not to leave the family business in Edinburgh, while Robert established his own practice in London assisted by his younger brother James. William Adam, the youngest brother, never travelled in Europe but through William Adam and Company (established in 1764) continued his father's merchant business as a major supplier of building materials.

A Grand Tour

Robert Adam was twenty-six years old when he left for Rome in October 1754. Travelling initially with his brother James as far as Lille, he met up with the Hon. Charles Hope in Brussels. Robert wrote regularly to his brothers and sisters with a frankness and sincerity that might seem more appropriate to a personal journal. For example, on 13 February 1755, eleven days before their arrival in Rome, he writes home of the Florence Carnival where, with Charles Hope, he danced through the night 'with all the Greatest Quality and with Some of the

Hopetoun House, Edinburgh, where the Adam brothers' work on the interior followed their father's remodelling of the exterior. Engraving from Vitruvius Scoticus *(by courtesy of the Trustees of Sir John Soane's Museum).*

greatest Whores and with the Handsomest of both kinds wherever I could get at them.'

Travelling with Hope provided entrée to society at a higher level than a professional might enjoy, but Adam remained painfully aware of his relative social standing. He wrote home: 'If I am known in Rome to be an Architect, if I am seen drawing or with a pencil in my hand, I cannot enter into genteel company, who will not admitt an Artist, or if they do admitt him, will very probably rub affronts on him, in order to prevent his appearing at their Card playing, Balls or Concerts.' He even asked James 'You will always take care to avoid putting the word Architect on the back of my letters. You shou'd either Direct "For Rob' Adam. Esq." or "A Mon^r, Robert Adam, Gentil'homme Anglois".'

In Florence, Adam met the sculptor Joseph Wilton and the French architect Charles-Louis Clérisseau. The Frenchman later produced designs for Catherine the Great, but at this early stage in his career (his Prix de Rome scholarship from the Academie in Paris had ended in 1754) Clérisseau was content to serve as Adam's antiquarian guide and teacher of watercolour and draughtsmanship, in exchange for his board. He had studied under Panini, the fashionable painter of Rome's classical buildings. Adam wrote of him: 'He raised my Ideas, he created emulation and fire in my Breast, I wish'd above all things to learn his manner and have him with me at Rome, to study close with him.'

Clérisseau taught Adam how to look, and to contain his ambition to design until he had wholly absorbed the qualities of classical architecture. As he wrote to James: 'Clérisseau preaches to me every day to forbear inventing or composing either plans or Elevations till I have a greater fund, that is, till I have made more progress in seeing things and my head more filled with proper ornaments…'.

Charles, Lord Hope, his brother the Hon. James Hope and their tutor William Rouet in Rome, by Nathaniel Dance, 1763. (Pilgrim Press Ltd, Derby; in the private collection of Lord Linlithgow and on display at Hopetoun House, South Queensferry)

Adam travelled to Rome with Clérisseau and Hope, and soon parted company with his aristocratic companion, preferring detailed study of buildings and monuments to operas, dinners and balls. The best of both worlds was not possible if he was to succeed as an architect. For a younger brother of a Scottish earl, the Grand Tour might be the chance of a lifetime to enjoy international society to the full before settling in Britain, but for the younger brother of a Scottish architect, it had to be the foundation of a career. However, Adam's taste for high life did not leave with Hope. He travelled in considerable comfort, and his resolve in 1755 to be 'as frugal as possible' in reality meant employing not only Clérisseau, but a cook, valet, coachman and valet *de pace* ('for going Errands and behind the Coach'). Small wonder that in the

The Piazza del Pantheon, one of many drawings made by Robert Adam in Rome.
(Royal Commission on Ancient Monuments, Scotland/Sir John Clerk Collection)

Neapolitan village of Attina Robert and Clérisseau were mistaken for English princes.

Rome left Adam breathless. For an architect in the neoclassical era, it was the promised land. He wrote home on his arrival in 1755: 'Rome is the most glorious place in the Universal World. A Grandeur, a tranquillity reigns in it. Every where noble and striking remains of antiquity appear in it.' Here Robert would be able to study at first hand the great sources of Palladio, whose influence had so dominated eighteenth-century British architecture.

Rome's classical and Renaissance buildings provided a catalogue of the finest sources for an aspiring architect, and hundreds of drawings made by Adam in Rome survive. But at the same time, Rome was a hive of students, home to a generation of potential rivals. Sixteen British architects were in Rome between 1753 and 1757, including Robert Mylne, Matthew Brettingham the Younger, James Wyatt and William Chambers.

Soon after arriving in Rome Adam recognized the genius of Chambers, and revealed in his letters his impassioned determination to outshine all his contemporaries: 'Chambers is a more formidable foe . . . whither I shall be able to stand my ground against him when I am there [ie back in England] is really what I cannot determine.' Just ten days after his arrival in Rome on 24 February 1755 he wrote to his sister Peggy of Chambers: 'But damn my Blood but I will have a fair tryal for it, and expect to do as much in Six months, as he has done in as many Years.'

Some idea of the scale of Adam's youthful ambition is provided by his *Design for a Palace* of 1757, a drawing itself measuring over 9 feet in length. The grandiose scale of the palace is not to be taken literally, for the design belongs to a genre of architectural draughtsmanship then popular among competing students in Italy. Essentially it defines a vision of future glory, of the architect at the gateway to his new career, fired by enthusiasm and self-confidence.

Behind this colossal fantasy of architectural erudition lay the influence of another friendship formed in Italy. Adam had met the Venetian draughtsman Giovanni Battista Piranesi in June 1755. Their admiration was mutual, as Adam wrote on 21 June 1755:

Piranesi who is I think the most extraordinary fellow I ever saw is become immensely intimate with me and as he imagined at first sight that I was like the other Englishes who had love for Antiques without knowledge, upon seeing some of my Sketches and Drawings, was so highly delighted that he almost ran quite distracted and says that I have more genius for the true noble architecture than any Englishman ever was in Italy.

Piranesi championed Rome against the growing claims for Greece as the true source of classical art and architecture. Adam also knew proponents of the opposite view in the debate, and through Clérisseau encountered some of the era's most advanced thinking on architecture. However, his attitude to the antique did not become consumed by current controversies, nor did he collect as a gentleman to adorn a country house. Instead, Adam saw the antique, primarily, as architectural source material, to be measured, sketched, cast and, if possible, purchased, and he employed draughtsmen, painters and mould makers to record anything of potential use as well as sketching himself. Adam recognized that the masters of the Renaissance were able to study antique remains in better condition two centuries before him and he took a particular interest in *grotesque* ornament (named after *grotte* from its derivation from Roman decoration found in vaulted ruins) which Adam studied in the Vatican *Loggie* and the Villa Madama. Herculaneum provided him with further evidence of the decoration of domestic architecture, and fuelled his growing conviction of the inappropriateness of the Palladian style to British houses.

The Journey to 'Spalatro'

Adam hoped to visit Greece and, if funds permitted, Egypt and the Holy Land, but by the summer of 1757 only one more expedition seemed feasible. In his desire to research further the domestic architecture of ancient Rome, Adam set out with his draughtsmen for 'Spalatro' (Spalato, later Split, in Dalmatia) and one of the best preserved palaces built for a Roman Emperor.

Diocletian's luxury seafront *palatium* covered 9½ acres and envelops the later town (to which it gave its name) like a fortress. It was built around AD305 when Diocletian abdicated and had never been published.

Detail from Robert Adam's Design for a Palace, 1757. The drawing's scale and ambition reveal Adam's love of self-advertisement, and his (unfulfilled) ambition to design a major public building, such as a palace for George III. (By courtesy of the Trustees of Sir John Soane's Museum)

Adam must have been driven by the need not only to research source material for his own designs, but to establish his qualifications as a scholar, alongside those of an artist and connoisseur.

Clérisseau had been working for Adam on a proposed new edition of *Les Edifices antiques de Rome* by Antoine Desgodetz (first published in 1682) with the intention of publishing the corrected measurements in red ink, as Robert Adam recorded 'which lets them see the error'. Clérisseau's energies were now switched full time to recording the Palace. Helped by two assistants, the team completed the project of measuring the palace and producing perspective views in just five weeks, in July and August 1757. Clérisseau later supervised the engraving of the plates in Venice with James Adam and indeed, Robert Adam's *Ruins of the Palace of the Emperor Diocletian, at Spalatro, in Dalmatia* might equally be credited to Clérisseau. It finally appeared in 1764.

A truly European production, it consists of 61 views of the palace and measured drawings of the architectural details by four Italians and a Frenchman (Bartolozzi, Santini, Cunego, Zucchi and Clérisseau) with a descriptive text by Robert Adam. The list of over 500 subscribers is headed by Frederick the Great, King of Prussia (Britain's ally in the Seven Year's War) to whom a complimentary copy was sent. The 28 foreign subscribers include the Venetian Ambassador and the Library of St Mark at Venice. This list reads like a boastful advertisement of Adam's friends and clients, and includes nearly half of the clients of his rival, William Chambers. By the time the volume appeared, six years after his return to England, Adam had become the most fashionable architect in London. In case anyone might be in doubt, the list of patrons was there to underline Adam's reputation at home and abroad. Today the list makes one wonder whether subscribers used such lavish volumes to demonstrate their awareness of

recent archaeology, and of the latest sources of modern design.

In his text Adam describes the expedition and the hurdles the team had to surmount, such as the Venetian governor who was convinced that they were Turkish spies. He also includes a brief treatise of his ideas on design and planning. Adam claimed that the volume contained 'the only full and accurate designs that have hitherto been published of any private Edifice of the Ancients' and that the palace formed the basis of his ideas for domestic buildings. In fact, whilst its influence may be traced in his work at Syon House, Luton Hoo, Kedleston and particularly the riverfront terrace of the Adelphi, as Sir John Summerson has pointed out, Spalatro gave Adam less source material than Robert Wood's *Ruins of Palmyra* (1753) and *Ruins of Baalbek* (1757), or Le Roy's *Ruines des plus Beaux Monuments de la Grèce* (1758).

The volume is dedicated to George III whose patronage for a great palace it clearly sought to inspire. The dedication invites the young king to admire:

> the favourite residence of a great Emperor, who, by his Munificence and Example, revived the Study of Architecture. . . . At this happy Period, when Great Britain enjoys in Peace the Reputation and Power she acquired by Arms, Your Majesty's singular Attention to the Arts of Elegance promises an Age of Perfection that will compleat the Glories of Your Reign, and fix an AEra no less remarkable than that of PERICLES, AUGUSTUS or the MEDICIS.

Unfortunately, the volume failed to inspire commissions from the courts of Europe, and when a copy was presented to the newly formed Royal Academy in 1769 via its first treasurer, William Chambers, it failed to prompt Adam's election as an Academician. Compared to Adam's *Works in Architecture* it has been relatively passed over in Adam studies, and yet, while *Spalatro* was not a major influence on the 'Adam style' it is crucial to an understanding of Robert Adam's ambitions, the planning of his domestic buildings, and

Diocletian's Palace at Spalato from the sea, from Robert Adam's Ruins of …Spalatro, *1764. Adam claimed that the palace formed the basis of his ideas for domestic architecture, a claim which later gave rise to criticism that his ideas were based on 'degenerate' late Roman architecture (see page 48). (National Library of Scotland)*

the way in which, aided by his brothers, he carefully promoted his own career.

After completing work at 'Spalatro' Adam returned to Venice, and on 12 October 1757 wrote to his agents: 'I am on my departure from Italy as my creditors come so hard upon me; However, there is no remedy for it.' By January 1758 he was back in England, ready to launch his own practice in London.

The Effect of Italy

The architect who returned from Italy had matured considerably from the pleasure-seeking companion of the Hon. Charles Hope of over three years before. Approaching his thirtieth birthday, Adam had now established a lead over his brothers which he was never to relinquish. He had acquired the necessary qualifications both of a gentleman of taste and of a professional architect. A newly elected member of the principal artistic academies of Italy, he was in a position to converse at least on equal terms with dilettante patrons, sharing their international tastes and memories of the golden days of the Grand Tour. He must have recognized the associative appeal that the Adam style could offer as unlimited souvenirs and as settings for Italian marbles and paintings in British homes. Through his conversations with artists and writers he had encountered the most controversial architectural theories of the age. His research at Diocletian's palace had given him an exclusive knowledge of Roman architecture, one which, as yet unpublished, might be shared with the most generous patrons, who wished to stay one step ahead of fashion.

Adam returned armed not only with a repertoire of classical and Renaissance ornament, but with a new inspiration for the architecture of Britain. His vision was based, not on ancient public buildings measured at second hand from sixteenth-century Italian pattern books, but rather on a direct, personal response to both the public and domestic architecture of Imperial Rome.

Patrons and Practice

The London Office

Potential may be glorious but it remains unrealized without the practical wherewithal to capitalize on opportunities. Robert Adam's genius took various forms. Alongside his great gifts and knowledge, a handful of more prosaic, worldly abilities must be recognized if we are to understand how, within three years of his return from Rome, he had become Britain's most fashionable architect.

In Rome Adam had evaluated the competition he would face if he were to practise in London rather than return to the family business in Edinburgh. Lord Burlington's generation of Palladian architects had passed (Burlington died in 1753, Gibbs in 1754, Kent in 1748 and Leoni in 1746) but their tradition continued. Despite the controversies in Rome over the relative merits of Greek and Roman architecture, and the alternatives offered in England by the lingering Rococo taste for 'Gothick' and 'Chinoiserie', no 'Battle of the Styles' raged, such as occurred a century later.

According to Thomas Hardwicke, the neo-Palladians James Paine (c.1716–89) and Robert Taylor (1714–88) 'nearly divided the practice of the profession between them for they had few competitors till Mr Robert Adam entered the lists'. John Carr (1723–1807) was their most distinguished rival. Matthew Brettingham the Younger (1725–1803) Adam had dismissed in Rome but Robert Mylne (1734–1811), a fellow Scot, was to return from Rome in 1759, having won First Prize at the Accademia di S. Luca the previous year, and by 1760 Mylne was designing Blackfriars' Bridge. James 'Athenian' Stuart (1713–88) had visited Greece in 1751–5, was preparing his *Antiquities of Athens* (1762) for publication with Nicholas Revett, and from 1760 was designing rooms for Spencer House. But Adam knew that his greatest rival had to be William Chambers (1723–96). Chambers had studied in Paris under Blondel in 1749, in Italy from 1750–55, and had established his practice in London in 1755. The following year he had secured royal favour through his appointment as architectural tutor to the Prince of Wales. Something extra was needed if Adam was to make his claim to preeminence over such competition.

Robert Adam had a natural ability which today would be termed 'marketing'. Determined to attract the most fashionable clients, he initially rented a fu͡ ͡ hed house in St James's Place with six servants. James Adam reported to one of their sisters 'Bob still continues to pay his respects to the great as he has now got a place for showing his things, he is ready to admit strangers'. Naturally, some self-indulgence also lay behind this ostentatious lifestyle, but it would have made a sharp contrast with that of Chambers who, James noted, lived 'in a poor mean lodging up a long dark stair'.

Soon after, Robert purchased a house in Lower Grosvenor Street, and two of his sisters arrived to take care of his household. Jenny and Betty were later joined by Peggy. The importance of Adam's family to his successful rise in London cannot be underestimated. His sisters are the unsung heroines: moving from Edinburgh to London, they added to the security already provided to the young bachelor by his older brother's financial support. Presumably they were also there to safeguard John's investment. Robert had hoped to remain John's partner in practice, but his brother agreed to provide this support only for a year, and lent him the capital to buy his Mayfair premises.

James might have proved a rival but enjoyed his Grand Tour in 1760–63, just when Robert was attracting clients and so establishing his dominance over the family. Although James spent slightly longer on his tour (1760–63), had more servants and draughtsmen and visited Pompeii and Paestum, he succumbed to the temptations Robert had resisted, and was regarded by Clérisseau as a snobbish dandy. He was to become the administrator of the London practice, and their younger brother William the financial manager.

Adam's swift rise can also be partly credited to the support he received from his assistants and craftsmen. Already in Italy Adam had revealed his gift for recognizing international talent, in his choice of Clérisseau and Piranesi as friends and tutors, and of engravers for the *Spalatro* volume. In England he employed gifted craftsmen who were willing to execute his designs without aspiring to outshine him as creative artists. Most noted today are the painters Zucchi, Rebecca and Cipriani, the sculptors Thomas Carter and Michael Spang, and the plasterer Joseph Rose; Angelica Kauffmann and William Hamilton are the exceptions in attaining independent fame. The cabinet makers William France and John Linnell realized many of Adam's designs for furniture.

The Scotch Connection

French, Italian, Flemish, German and Russian craftsmen all worked for Adam's international team, but in seeking patrons Adam readily reasserted his northern origins.

Foremost of the Scots to achieve prominence in London in Adam's time was John Stuart, 3rd Earl of Bute. After serving as tutor to George III when Prince of Wales, Bute became the King's First Minister in 1761, and was soon accused of appointing fellow Scots to positions vacated by Whigs. In 1756 Bute, as principal adviser to the Princess of Wales, mother of the heir-apparent,

appointed William Chambers as architectural tutor to the young prince. Word must have reached Adam in Rome, and the following year Adam sought an introduction to Bute via the 'bluestocking' Lady Mary Wortley Montagu. In January 1758 Lady Mary wrote from Rome to her daughter, Lady Bute: 'I saw, some months ago, a countryman of yours (Mr Adam) who desires to be introduced to you. He seemed to me, in one short visit, to be a man of genius, and I have heard his knowledge of architecture much applauded. He is now in England.' In May Adam's friend John Home, now Bute's secretary, arranged an introduction for the architect, together with his fellow Scots William Robertson and Dr Alexander Carlyle.

Bute received the three Scotsmen in some haste, and once outside, according to Carlyle, Adam 'fell a-cursing and swearing. What! had he been presented to all the princes in Italy and France, and most graciously received, to come and be treated with such distance and pride by the youngest earl but one in Scotland!' His self-esteem took a further blow when Bute returned a book which Adam had sent. In August 1758 Adam wrote to a friend of this second sleight, referring to Bute's intimacy with the Princess of Wales:

> Then h[e]is returning me that Book of Piranesi's was another private and masterly stroke. He kept it for 3 months till he got intelligence of some more copies coming by another ship from Italy when he instantly bought one of from David Wilson and return'd me mine. . . . I shall certainly be revenged on Bute for this conduct. I have a great mind to go out to K-[Kew] and when he and Madam P [the Princess of Wales] are living together, I'll have them put in a boat naked and brought down the river like Adam & Eve, and I'll fell him dead with Piranesi's 4 folio volumes from Westminster Bridge as they are going to pass under the Yoke & Robt. Adam. If you disapprove, write me a better scheme.

Fortunately, Adam's plot remained unhatched as Bute in fact proved instrumental in the architect's rise. The year after the accession of George III Bute appointed Adam 'Joint Architect of his Majesty's Works' with Chambers. In 1762 he commissioned Adam to build 'Bute House' in Berkeley Square (sold in 1765, before completion, to Lord Shelburne) and in the same year purchased Luton Hoo, which Adam remodelled from 1767. When the *Spalatro* volume appeared in 1764 the subscribers' list revealed that ten copies had been assigned to Bute. He later commissioned Adam to build Highcliffe. Bute had lived at Kenwood, which he sold in 1754 to another fellow Scot, William Murray, later Lord Mansfield, and in 1764 Mansfield commissioned the Adam brothers to remodel and extend Kenwood.

Robert Adam associated with the growing number of 'North Britons' who seemed to dominate government, the Courts and medicine in London in the 1760s. Political ambitions may have lain behind some of Adam's early commissions and his entering Parliament in 1768, but Adam shielded any such motivations against the growing antipathy towards the influx of Scots in London. Clear benefits to business were to be had by an architect entering Parliament, even beyond the 'inside advantage' over his rivals of ready introductions to potential patrons as their social equal. For example, legislation had to be steered through Parliament before the brothers could drain and enclose the muddy bay in the Thames on which they would build the Adelphi. When this speculative development brought them to the brink of bankruptcy, they successfully petitioned Parliament in 1773 for permission to dispose of their assets by lottery. Robert Adam left the House of Commons the following year but in 1776 he still held enough influence to obtain an Act of Parliament authorizing the brothers alone to manufacture 'Adam's new invented patent stucco'. Two years later the manufacturer of an improved stucco compositon was brought to trial before Lord Mansfield who, judging

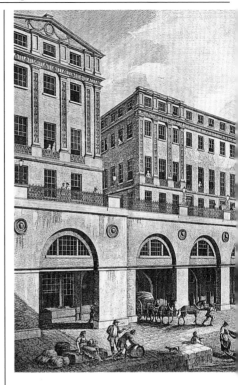

the case in favour of his fellow Scots, unwittingly prompted renewed suspicions and dislike of the Adam brothers.

English Patronage

Among the various factors which help to explain Robert Adam's rapid rise in London, the initial contribution of Scottish contacts and patrons must have been the most decisive. But he was far from dependent upon an expatriate clientele. The central decade of his career, between the publication of the *Spalatro* volume in 1764 and the appearance of the first part of the brothers' *Works in Architecture* in 1773, coincided with a period of peace and prosperity in Britain. During this decade of opportunity Adam executed the commissions with which he is most often

The Adelphi, London: Royal Terrace, facing the Thames, from Adam's Works. *This speculative development behind the Strand brought the Adam brothers to the brink of bankruptcy.*

identified today: Syon, Kedleston, Harewood, Kenwood, Osterley, Nostell Priory and Newby Hall.

Ironically, despite the enormous wealth available, Adam was not in demand for building new country houses, but for completing, or remodelling earlier ones. On occasions he followed hard on the heels of his rivals, and outshone them. For example, he succeeded Carr of York at Harewood; at Kedleston, Nostell Priory, Alnwick Castle and Syon James Paine (whom he initially preceded at Kedleston); at Bowood Henry Keene and at Osterley William Chambers. He also remodelled much earlier buildings, for Syon was a Tudor house, Osterley Elizabethan, and Kenwood (originally) Jacobean, while Newby Hall dates from the 1690s.

English patronage was not prompted simply by the fashion for neoclassical decoration and the novelty of employing Adam's repertoire of antique motifs. A gradual change in social customs, particularly in the reception of visitors and guests, necessitated more inventive planning of houses, which Adam could provide. The straight hierarchy of chambers found in many seventeenth- and early eighteenth-century houses now seemed awkward to guests who expected a more varied circuit with different room types, shapes and decoration. Each room could be appropriate to a different diversion such as cards, conversation, supper or dancing, activities which might all take place at the same time. Such a circuit might lead around a stairhall and even link with the gardens outside. Visitor routes, room

Kedleston Hall, Derbyshire; the marble hall by Robert Adam, c.1760–68. At Kedleston, Robert Adam succeeded two of his rivals, Brettingham and Paine, and was responsible for the south front (see page 51) as well as interiors. (A F Kersting)

functions and floor plans had to be revised, not just surfaces redecorated, if family seats were to become fashionable and comfortable without being demolished and rebuilt. Adam recognized the desire for continuity between generations and understood the potential of such patronage if vast sums could be spent on refurbishing, rather than on rebuilding.

Less familiar today than Adam's country houses but perhaps more interesting are the Mayfair town houses Adam built in the 1770s, most notably Derby House in Grosvenor Square, Wynn House in St James's Square, Lansdowne House in Berkeley Square, and Home House in Portman Square. Adam may have been a generation late for building new country houses but he took full advantage of the market for urban palaces available in the fashionable West End of London as a result of the migration from the City. He relished the chance to design suites for grand receptions from scratch. Far from being modest *pieds-à-terre* for country landowners, these elegant residences were to become London's answer to the *hôtels* of Paris and the noble palaces of Rome, Florence and Genoa. Here

hostesses could compete during the London season, when Parliament was in session. Ever new heights of fashion had to be reached, and ingenious solutions discovered, to make the most of limited space. Lessons learnt by Adam in remodelling and extending country houses were readily applied to enhance the pleasures of London society.

The one area of potential patronage Adam may have misjudged was in the speculative building of London terraces. He undertook six speculative projects in London, of which the Adelphi scheme is the best known today. This development between the Strand and the Thames included 69 houses, but it failed financially after the Government declined to lease the basement level warehousing for fear of flooding. Immediate competition from James Paine's adjacent development in Salisbury Street and the Strand was also to blame; all 26 of Paine's properties were let by 1773, a year before the Adam brothers held a lottery to avoid bankruptcy. Most of the Adelphi was demolished in 1936, but Portland Place (1773–8) and Fitzroy Square (1790–1800)

Portland Place, London; the eastern elevation. Although the earliest designs for Portland Place are signed by James Adam, Robert is credited with the general concept of a British 'Strada di Palazzi'. (By courtesy of the Trustees of Sir John Soane's Museum)

give some idea of Adam's cosmopolitan vision of London before Nash, with terraces designed to resemble palaces.

The terrace houses of Portland Place and Fitzroy Square lack the detail of Robert

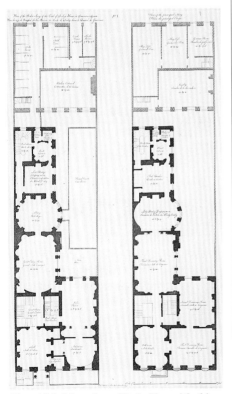

The published floor plans of Derby House, Mayfair (1773–4) reveal Adam's ingenious solutions to the difficulties of orchestrating society receptions within the confines of town houses.

Adam's commissioned work, for they were put up to sell, by builders working to the architects' designs. Crucial to the success of these speculative schemes was the attraction of suitable first residents. For example, David Garrick moved into 6 Royal Terrace at the Adelphi, with Robert Adam at number 4 and the premises of the Society of Arts behind in John Street. In Mansfield Street, laid out from 1770–73, early clients included Lord Scarsdale, Adam's patron at Kedleston. The centrepiece of the west side of Portland Place, Stormont House, was occupied in 1779 by Viscount Stormont, nephew and heir of Lord Mansfield, Adam's patron at Kenwood. But the loyalty of Adam's friends and patrons was not enough to guarantee a profitable stake in the growth of London's West End.

In the last decade of Adam's life Scottish patronage became crucial once again, particularly in Edinburgh where the need to stem the exodus of young professionals to London contributed to the building of the New Town. Charlotte Square (designed 1791) is a posthumous, partial realization of Adam's scheme, but Edinburgh also provided Adam with the opportunity to design public buildings. The Register House (c.1772–92) and the University (1788–92) were his chance to design on the grand scale and the closest he came to fulfilling aspirations expressed in Rome and in the dedication of the *Spalatro* volume. The causes of Adam's failure to secure a major royal commission and of his decline from fashionable favour in England from the mid 1770s will be explored below.

Luton Hoo, Bedfordshire: decoration for the drawing room and stairs, published in Robert and James Adam's Works, *1775. 'Luton Park' followed Syon House and Kenwood as the third part of the brothers' catalogue of commissions.*

Adam's Works

Prefaces and Principles

Adam's *Works* began to appear in parts from 1773, and now need to be considered if we are to appreciate the principles behind his achievements. Like the *Spalatro* volume, the publication indicates a factor crucial to Robert's early success: his continuing recognition of the importance of publicity. It also opens a new chapter in Adam's career, as the architect, aged 45, takes stock of a decade of successful commissions. Far from being complacent he is aware of new rivals, financial pressures, and of old ambitions still unfulfilled.

Appreciations of Adam's achievement tend to focus on a particular selection of country houses, namely Syon, Saltram, Harewood, Kedleston, Osterley, Newby Hall and Nostell Priory. In addition to their quality and importance, these houses have become synonymous with Adam because they are still largely intact, retain their original furnishings, have suffered relatively little architectural alteration by later generations, and are open to the public. However, with the exception of Syon and a passing reference to Kedleston, none of these houses features in *The Works in Architecture of Robert and James Adam*. The commissions chosen for inclusion in the *Works* provide the best guide to Robert Adam's achievement as he saw it.

The full text to the *Works* is another relatively undervalued resource, for it describes particular commissions as illustrations of architectural principles. As such the *Works* also presents Adam's claim to recognition as a man of thought.

The first volume appeared in parts from 1773, and is dated on the title page 1778. Essentially it consists, like the *Spalatro* volume, of large engravings, some of the best by Piranesi and Zucchi. The five parts of volume one are devoted, in turn, to the brothers' designs for Syon, Kenwood, Luton Park (today known as Luton Hoo), Public Buildings and 'Designs for the King and Queen, and the Princess Dowager of Wales etc'.

Volume two appeared in parts from 1777 and balances the discussion of three country houses in the first volume with three London town houses: Derby House, Wynn House and Shelburne (later Lansdowne) House. The fourth part of volume two continues the account of Syon House and the fifth, devoted to 'Public and Private Buildings', includes three views of Mistley Church, and two of the Theatre Royal. The third volume, which appeared posthumously in 1822, amounts to a publisher's miscellany of engravings not used in the earlier editions.

The *Works* discussed are credited to both Robert and James, but the publication itself is generally regarded today as Robert's achievement. Various comments are written by him in the first person singular and relate to sets of designs stated as being by Robert Adam alone. James Adam regarded himself as something of an architectural theorist and the first Preface repeats an unpublished essay he wrote in Rome in 1762 following correspondence with the Scottish judge and philosopher Lord Kames. However, we may assume that his ideas were evolved with his brother Robert before he left for Italy. Indeed, the Adam style was defined in designs and buildings by the older brother before James returned to England in 1763.

Various remarks in the text reveal that an even more ambitious publication had been planned; the subjects of the engravings and their dates similarly indicate a change in direction after they had been commissioned. The steady decrease in the amount of text underlines this sense of any initial structure fading away, and of the architects' commitment to the project being undermined by the pressures of architectural commissions.

The publication belongs to an architects' tradition dating back to Vitruvius's *de Architectura*, the classic architectural treatise consisting of ten books, dedicated to Emperor Augustus in 25BC. *Vitruvius Britannicus*, a collection of designs for modern buildings compiled by Colen Campbell, appeared from 1715; supplementary volumes by Woolfe and Gandon were published in 1769 and 1771 and included designs by Robert Adam. William Adam, the brothers' father, produced *Vitruvius Scoticus* (a work devoted mainly to his own designs, but including buildings by other architects) which did not appear as a single volume until 1810.

Competition was a driving factor in the creation of the *Works*. Despite all the achievements of the previous decade the brothers could not relax. In addition to Chambers and Paine (who had each published treatises and designs, in 1759 and 1767 respectively), there lay the prospect of a new generation of rivals, most notably James Wyatt, twenty years Robert's junior, who shot to fame in London in 1770 with the opening of the Pantheon in Oxford Street, when he was twenty-three. Builders following the brothers' designs in speculative ventures and mere imitators of fashion threatened to degrade the true 'Adam style', clouding the quality of the brothers' actual commissions. The architects needed to reclaim and celebrate their genuine works, in a selective *catalogue raisonnée* of their achievements to date if they were not to be judged by the work of their followers. As a landscape painter himself Robert Adam may well have had in mind how the seventeenth-century French painter Claude Lorrain recorded his pictures in his *Liber veritatis* as a safeguard against forgeries.

Another clear motive for the *Works* was to attract publicity and hence patrons for the practice. Nearly a decade had passed since the impact of the *Spalatro* volume, and still the brothers lacked a substantial royal commission, at home or abroad. The bilingual text, in English and French, indicates their international aspirations, whilst the range of commissions chosen (despite the original preoccupation with Syon House) demonstrated their versatility. One reason for the omission of the great country houses by which Robert Adam is usually judged today, besides the need to show this variety of experience, may be their relative distance from London society, unlike Syon, Kenwood and Luton Hoo. As the homes of the Duke of Northumberland, Lord Mansfield and Lord Bute these three houses would also have been of interest in their own right. They had the further distinction of being fresh commissions, where the architects were not succeeding their rivals.

A more noble motivation behind the *Works* should also be credited to the brothers. Now in their forties, they were in a mature position to expound their theories in a manifesto. The *Works* repay close reading, for beyond the visual principles of the 'Adam style' there lies a wealth of period ideas on the nature of architecture.

'A kind of revolution'

The first part of the *Works*, devoted to Syon, includes a much quoted preface summarizing the brothers' achievement to date as they saw it and setting out their key principles. They claimed 'to have brought about in this country, a kind of revolution in the whole system of this useful and elegant art' without having 'trod in the path of others'. Unfortunately such bold claims suggest more a sense of insecurity than of self satisfaction. Against the academic allegiance to the classical orders of architecture the brothers defend the freedom of the creative artist, believing 'the great masters of antiquity were not so rigidly scrupulous, they varied the proportions as the general spirit of their

The Sculpture Gallery at Newby Hall, North Yorkshire, 1767, illustrates well Adam's notion of 'movement' in architecture, as described in the Works. *This characteristic of the 'Adam style' involves an interplay of contrasting shapes, light and shadow that is indebted to landscape painting and to the architecture of Vanbrugh and William Kent. The Sculpture Gallery is one of two wings added by Adam at Newby, where he also altered the interiors of the main rooms. (A F Kersting)*

composition required'. It is this general spirit of antiquity that the brothers feel they have succeeded in seizing, particularly by avoiding the repetition of over-familiar classical features:

> The massive entablature, the ponderous compartment ceiling, the tabernacle frame, almost the only species of ornament formerly known, in this country, are now universally exploded, and in their place, we have adopted a beautiful variety of light mouldings, gracefully formed, delicately enriched and arranged with propriety and skill. We have introduced a great diversity of ceilings, freezes, and decorated pilasters, and have added grace and beauty to the whole, by a mixture of grotesque stucco, and painted ornaments together with the flowing rainceau, with its fanciful figures and winding foliage.

Fundamental to their 'revolution' is a belief in a clear difference between external and internal decoration in classical architecture and between public and private buildings, which they feel has passed unnoticed hitherto. In 'temples and other public works . . . the ancients . . . kept of a bold and massive style. . . .

> But on the inside of their edifices the ancients were extremely careful to proportion both size and depth of their compartments and pannels, to the distance from the eye and the objects with which they were to be compared; and, with regard to the decoration of their private and bathing apartments, they were all delicacy, gaiety, grace, and beauty.

This basic distinction, the brothers believed, was misunderstood by the Renaissance masters: 'from this mistake of the first modern Italian artists, all Europe has been misled, and has been servilely groaning under this load for these three centuries past'. Once the basic flaw of the European tradition has been recognized, the brothers' designs may serve as a corrective treatise, 'to point out a new stile of composition for those parts of interior decoration'.

A typical example of Adam's 'grotesque' ornament (so named because of its derivation from the decoration found in vaulted Roman ruins or grotte*), in the Little Drawing Room at Audley End, Essex.*

Two characteristics of the Adam style are introduced before illustration through their commissions: *movement* and *grotesque* ornament. Both underline the claim for the taste of the creative artist above any academic imitation of measured details, and remind us today that neoclassicism does not directly equate with classical sources, symmetry and stability.

'Movement' is a love of contrasts in light, shade, and shape, whether in the overall form of buildings, details of a facade, or sequence of rooms. It seeks to apply the aesthetic theories of the picturesque from painting and landscape gardening to architecture. The brothers uphold two works by the baroque architect Vanbrugh: 'Blenheim and Castle Howard as great examples of these perfections' even though 'his works are so crowded with barbarisms and absurdities . . . that none but the discerning can separate their merits from their defects'. Only two other British architects are praised elsewhere in this preface: William Kent (although his works are 'those of a beginner') and James 'Athenian' Stuart.

The application of 'movement' to the plan and elevation of buildings should not be credited to the Adam brothers alone. Indoors both Robert Taylor and James Paine explored the potential of a more varied, even elastic, sense of space through the use of octagonal, circular and apsidal-ended rooms, columnar screens and a variety of ceiling shapes. Their more obvious shared sources are Chiswick House by Kent and Burlington, Palladio's Palazzo Thiene and Palladio's reconstructions of Roman baths, as published by Burlington in 1730.

'Grotesque' ornament is a delicate style of Roman interior decoration known since Renaissance times when it was discovered in vaulted ruins. As so much had since been lost the brothers' preface recommends study of the early imitations by Raphael and his pupils in 'the loggias of the Vatican, the villas Madama, Parnfili, Caprarola, the old palace at Florence . . .' Another favoured form of interior decoration is '*Rainceau*, the winding and twisting of the stalk or stem of the acanthus plant . . . intertwined with human figures, animals and birds, imaginary or real; also with flowers and fruits'. Such principles the brothers sought to illustrate through the examples of their work.

Country Houses

The discussion of selected country houses in the *Works* is both an insight into Robert Adam's philosophy and a summary of what he aimed to achieve with these particular commissions. In particular, the section devoted to Syon illustrates Robert Adam's belief that architecture must contribute to 'the art of living'.

Syon House

Syon House, Middlesex is a Tudor building still owned, and opened to the public, by the Duke of Northumberland. Robert Adam remodelled and embellished Syon for over a decade from 1761. The difficulties set by working within a square building with varying floor levels and room heights might have defeated an architect of the Palladian school. To an architect in love with 'movement' these 'chief difficulties' proved to be an inspiration.

In all, twenty-four engravings relating to Syon appear in the three volumes of the

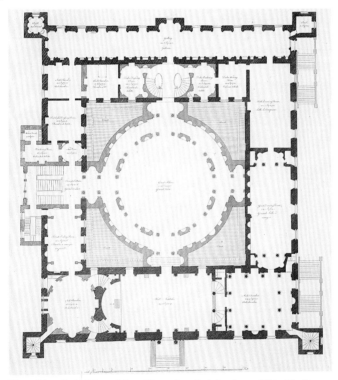

Plan of the principal floor of Syon House, Brentford, London, published in the Works *in 1773. The design of floor plans was described by the Adam brothers as 'one of those branches of our art, which has not hitherto been treated of with any accuracy, or studied with any care: though of all others, the most essential, both to the splendour and convenience of life'.*

Works, three times the number for each of
the other major commissions. Most of the text
relating to the engravings in volume one is
devoted to the floor plan. Discussion revolves
around the elegant style of living in the *hôtels*
of the French nobility, then considered to be
the height of fashion. The author asserts his
qualification to write on this subject: 'To
understand thoroughly the art of living, it is
necessary, perhaps, to have passed some time
amongst the French, and to have studied the
customs of that social and conversible people.'
Britain's shortcomings are compared to the
standards of French etiquette but the basic
premiss that the architecture of one country
cannot be copied slavishly in another is
upheld. Architecture must vary 'so as to
accommodate it to the manners of different
nations'.

The sequence of reception rooms at Syon
is a breathtaking progress through a series of
dramatic contrasts; the result is both highly
practical and visually astonishing. The
entrance hall 'of great dimension, is finished
with stucco, as halls always are, and is formed
with a recess at each end, one square and the
other circular'. One end leads to the private
apartments, the other, up a flight of steps, to
the reception suite. The latter begins with an
ante-room (see page 2). Rich and welcoming
with its wealth of colourful ornament it
appears to be a cube due to the use of
'columns of verd antique marble . . . which
standing insulated, serve to form the room
and heighten the scenery'. Screens of columns
are employed to equal effect in the 'great
eating-room' adjacent. Here Robert Adam
follows the French custom in decorating
dining rooms: 'Instead of being hung with
damask, tapestry,&c. they are always finished
with stucco, and adorned with statues and
paintings, that they may not retain the smell

*The entrance hall at Syon, designed in 1761, is articulated with robust classical ornament and furnished with
sculpture. The overall effect is both lavish and austere, providing an imposing start to a sequence of astonishing
contrasts. (A F Kersting)*

The Long Gallery at Syon House, from the Works. *Through the imaginative use of an erudite repertoire of ornament, the original, narrow Jacobean gallery has been articulated into a series of contrasting compartments. Each one presents an intimate medley of stucco decoration, paintings, sculpture or books, but is subtly linked with its neighbour and contributes to the unity of the vast room by the interlocking octagons running through the ceiling and carpet.*

of the victuals.' Next comes the withdrawing room, which 'prevents the noise of the men from being troublesome' to the ladies enjoying the gallery beyond after dinner.

The engraved perspective view of the gallery (published in volume three) provides the clearest summary of the Adam style in its early maturity, and illustrates in practice the principles upheld in the preface. In its variety of media and sense of unity the gallery illustrates the basic unwritten principle of the Adam style, that the architect must have total control over all aspects of interior design.

The sharp contrast between the sculptural conception of the entrance hall and the luxuriant complexities of the gallery have been seen as evidence of development within the Adam style, from its heavier Palladian

early phase. Primarily, however, it reveals Adam's concern for the practical and symbolic function of a space and its position, particularly in a reception suite where each room is conceived to play a strategic role in a hierarchy of mounting sensations.

The reception suite we enjoy at Syon today was almost marginal to Robert Adam's central ambition, a 'great circular saloon', inspired by the Pantheon, with which he had hoped to fill the inner courtyard. At the time of publication he expected to create this 'room of general rendezvous, and for public entertainments, with illuminations, dancing, and music. The form is new and singular . . . and leaves room for the imagination to play.' (He may equally have had in mind James Wyatt's sensational Pantheon in Oxford

The Library or Great Room at Kenwood, completed in 1770, is Robert Adam's best-known interior and provides a breathtaking summary of his abilities and ambitions.

Street.) Fortunately this ambition to break out of the constraints of remodelling earlier buildings and create a great saloon from scratch was to be realized a few miles north east from Syon while work proceeded there, namely at Kenwood.

Kenwood

The discussion of Syon in the *Works* focuses on room functions, their practical arrangement and appropriate decoration. The preface to the second part uses Kenwood to explore another specific theme in more detail, one which provides another insight into Robert Adam's breathtaking self-assurance.

The five Orders of classical architecture were then the subject of controversy. The brothers themselves

> acknowledge only three orders; the Doric, the Ionic, and the Corinthian: for as to the Tuscan it is, in fact, no more than a bad and imperfect Doric; and the Composite, or Roman Order, in our opinion, is a very disagreeable and awkward mixture of the Corinthian and Ionic.

At issue, however, is not any particular academic definition of classical proportions and ornament, but the very authority of the classical tradition over the creative genius of the living artist.

The brothers' contention was that the Orders, far from needing to be accurately codified into timeless rules, were there to be adjusted as the artist saw fit. Columns, capitals, entablatures and mouldings were not inviolate but ought to vary 'according to the style of the building where it is employed' and 'different circumstances of situation and propriety'. Variations could only be made, however, with 'the correct taste of the skilful and experienced artist', with a sense of excellence 'formed and improved by a correct taste, and diligent study'. By implication, men of great learning should step aside for the artist when it came to the appreciation of architecture – a notion which questioned the

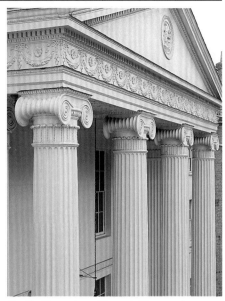

Detail of the portico at Kenwood, Hampstead, London, 1768–9.

traditional relationship in England between the architect as professional designer and builder, and the patron as gentleman connoisseur. Indeed, the initial acknowledgement of Robert Adam's patron at Kenwood, Lord Mansfield, goes beyond custom and effectively underlines the new relationship necessary if genius is to flourish: Lord Mansfield 'gave full scope to my ideas… I was at full liberty to make the proper deviations.' Robert Adam was commissioned to remodel the villa in the neoclassical taste, to insert a third storey and add a reception room that could also serve as a library.

Continuing the theme from the preface of the need to vary the orders to suit their setting, Adam vividly evokes Kenwood's remarkable location:

> Over the vale, through which the water flows, there is a noble view let into the house and terrace, of the city of London, Greenwich Hospital, the River Thames, the ships passing up and down, with an extensive prospect, but clear and distinct, on both sides of the river. To

Detail of the Kenwood Library ceiling. Adam explained that the use of colour in the panels surrounding the nineteen paintings by Zucchi was designed 'to relieve the ornaments, remove the crudeness of the white, and create a harmony between the ceiling and the sidewalls, with their hangings, pictures, and other decorations'.

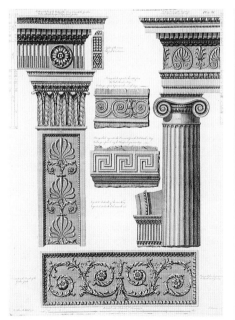

Details of the decoration used on the south front at Kenwood, from the Works *(1774).*

the north-east, and west of the house and terrace the mountainous villages of Highgate and Hampstead form delightful objects. The whole scene is amazingly gay, magnificent, beautiful, and picturesque. ...The decoration bestowed on this front of the house is suitable to such a scene. The idea is new, and has been generally approved.

The extensive use of stucco in the exterior decoration was ostensibly prompted by the need 'to conceal the brick-work, which being built at different times, was of various colours'. But it also gave Robert Adam his first opportunity to create a visual response to a landscape setting, and achieve unity in design between exterior and interior.

Inside, only the 'great Room' is described, but as at Syon principles of 'movement' will be found in the reception route to which it provides the fitting climax. The reader's interest in the library or great room is directed first to the use of mirrored recesses opposite the windows; these bring the 'extensive prospect' into the room itself. Next comes the use of column screens which serve, as in the Syon dining room, to separate the body of the room from the recesses at each end. The frieze running over the columns and around the room is not a standard classical quotation but is 'enriched' with lions and deer, the supporters and crest of Lord Mansfield's family arms.

The ceiling receives most discussion, both in its form and decoration. In contrast to the flat, white ceilings of the Palladian school, it

> is in the form and style of those of the ancients. It is an imitation of a flat arch, which is extremely beautiful, and much more perfect than that which is commonly called the coved ceiling. . . . which is a portion or quadrant of a circle around the room, and rising to a flat in the centre, seems to be altogether of modern invention.

In contrast to the vast ceiling paintings of the Italianate tradition criticised in the first preface, there are nineteen small paintings by Antonio Zucchi, surrounded by stucco work by Joseph Rose, the whole unified by a variety of pastel coloured grounds 'so as to take off the glare of white, so common in every ceiling, till of late'.

As in the previous number devoted to Syon, the final plate illustrates designs for furniture. The briefest of explanations is given but the engraving has become the best known image of British neoclassical furniture. It provides a visual summary of the Adam brother's versatility and principles of unity in design through the creative use of classical sources. Chambers and Stuart both designed furniture, but neither to the same extent as Adam.

Luton Hoo

The third and final country house to warrant inclusion in Adam's *Works* is Luton Hoo in Bedfordshire, which belonged to the Earl of Bute. It receives little attention in Adam literature as it was altered by Smirke in 1816,

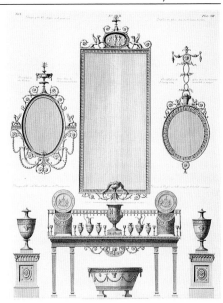

Furniture designed for Kenwood by Robert Adam, illustrated in the Works. *Sadly, Kenwood today lacks almost all its original contents as a consequence of the Kenwood auction in 1922, but a recent collection of Adam furniture complements the Iveagh Bequest of Old Master paintings.*

suffered an extensive fire in 1843 which destroyed most of the Adam interiors and was remodelled again in 1903. However, the account of Luton House (as it was then known) published by the Adam brothers in June 1774, provides a further key to their ideas.

The preface to this part lacks any ambitious claims of the type made earlier, but it contains three new issues. First, as most of the principal front of 'Luton House' lacked windows, Adam sought to make the most of the opportunity by 'introducing a kind of exterior decoration, which resembles that of a public work rather than of a private dwelling house'. Unfortunately his design for this west front was never realized. The advantages of giving 'an air of dignity and grandeur, of which few dwelling-houses are susceptible' was doubtless appropriate to the entrance of

Adam designed the entrance facade of Luton Hoo to resemble a public building. A similarly imposing effect was sought for Kenwood in the choice of the Erechtheion on the Acropolis in Athens as the source of the entrance portico. The Arch of Constantine and dome of the Pantheon are the direct sources for the south front of Kedleston.

the former prime minister's house, but it also indicates the brother's ambition to design public buildings, to which the following number is devoted.

Secondly, an engraving of internal architectural ornament (see page 22) pairs with the earlier illustration of details of Kenwood's south front. The explanation

Furniture designed for Luton Hoo. The brothers' text notes: 'The cornices for window curtains, with a great variety of other designs for this purpose, which we shall have occasion to give hereafter, were intended as an attempt to banish the absurd French compositions of this kind, heretofore so servilely imitated by the upholsterers of this country. ...The brass candelabra which stand in the niches of the drawing room were brought from abroad by the Earl of Bute, and ...are evidently the composition of some painter or statuary who has sacrificed the simple and the graceful to the busy and the picturesque.'

reinforces the same cry for 'latitude which the ancients took in compositions of this kind' rather than keeping decoration 'subjected to any of the customary rules'.

A third issue that emerges in the account of Luton House concerns furniture, the subject of the final engraving. The commentary here criticizes contemporary French and Italian designers and, by implication, the competition from imported goods. The architects' indirect appeal for patronage of native designers may seem inconsistent with their own employment of an international team of craftsmen, and their admiration of the French 'art of living'. However, it echoes the cry of British painters, at least since Hogarth, for an end to patrons' blind faith in the supremacy of foreign artists and their consequent neglect of British genius. This familiar lament is the theme of the two parts that follow in volume one, devoted to public buildings and royal commissions.

Public Buildings

Four public buildings were chosen for inclusion in the fourth part of the *Works*, published in January 1775: the Admiralty Screen in Whitehall, the 'Board-Room of the Paymaster-General and other Commissioners of Chelsea-Hospital', the premises of the Society of Arts in the Adelphi, and the Register Office in Edinburgh. The fifth part of volume two is devoted to the same subject and includes three engravings of Mistley Church in Essex, two of the Theatre Royal in Drury Lane and, by a stretch of the definition, the British Coffee-House in Cockspur Street. Edinburgh University features in the third, posthumous volume.

The brothers' modest tally of public buildings may come as a surprise, particularly if it is reduced to include only public commissions. The brief list highlights how the public face of Britain's capital was largely formed in the nineteenth century, but it also underlines the status of the brothers' rival, William Chambers, Surveyor General from 1782 and architect of Somerset House (1776–86). Nevertheless, the number of examples given in the *Works* contrasts with the choice of only three country houses from the many commissions the brothers received, and serves as a reminder of the way they hoped to be judged by patrons, critics and posterity.

Robert Adam's dream of designing and completing a public building of international importance is often seen as the personal aspiration of a highly ambitious man. However, in the *Works* he joins in the cry of British painters and sculptors of the era, in regarding such patronage as the rightful claim of artists in an age of empire and prosperity. It is not simply that

> such buildings must, of course, contain great and spacious apartments for the meeting of numerous assemblies; and, consequently, they are suspectible of more grandeur.

Rather, they are necessary to confirm the status of the nation, as a symptom of achievement beyond military and mercantile success. A footnote lists by way of comparison 'some of the principal buildings erected in the reign of Augustus' and concludes 'it was not possible the grandeur and decoration of public works could be neglected at a time when the ingenious Vitruvius lived, and the splendid Augustus reigned'.

Comparing commissions for private houses with enlightened patronage of public works, Adam draws a parallel with the schools of painting. The similarity is unstated, but he clearly regards public buildings as the architectural equivalent of history painting, that neglected genre held to be supreme by painters over the more imitative arts of portraiture and landscape painting by its appeal to the intellect. Unlike private houses where the 'repetition of windows . . . cuts the facade into minute parts' public buildings enable architects 'to preserve that greatness and simplicity of composition which, by imposing on the imagination, strikes the mind'.

The cry coincides with the views of James Barry (appointed Professor of Painting at the Royal Academy in 1782) in his *Inquiry into the Real and Imaginary Obstructions to the Acquisition of the Arts in England*, also published in 1775. Both echo the aspirations of the Society for the Encouragement of Arts, Manufactures, and Commerce, whose building by Adam is the subject of two plates in this number. In 1774 (the year before the Society finally signed the lease of its new premises in the Adelphi) the Society of Arts decided to commission historical and allegorical paintings to decorate its Great Room. The scheme followed the collapse of a long campaign to permit artists to decorate St Paul's Cathedral with paintings of religious subjects. In 1777 Barry began to paint, single handed, the astonishing historical cycle *The Progress of Human Culture* (completed 1784) that still adorns the Great Room of the Royal Society of Arts today.

Another close comparison with Adam's ideas, also published in 1775, is the sixth *Discourse to the Students of the Royal Academy* by its president, Joshua Reynolds. Devoted to the question of 'natural genius' versus the need for study, it includes a comparison of the Italian and Flemish schools of painting which is echoed in the brothers' fourth preface. After considering the ideal of designing public buildings against the actualities of creating 'ornamental decorations . . . in small rooms and private apartments' the *Works* draws a parallel between painting and architecture. It praises the Italian school for 'the greatness of their compositions ... the splendor and éclat of their general effect', and contrasts this with the Flemish artist's smallness of 'field', on which he achieves his 'exquisite and highly finished performance'.

Given that Robert Adam has been appreciated throughout the twentieth century primarily for his achievement inside country houses, it is sobering to recognise how he himself valued this aspect of his work as an architect. The brothers risk biting the hand that feeds them, after nearly two decades of commissions from private patrons, when the text contends that such private patronage is at the expense and to the neglect of public buildings. The implication is a political view of modern society as preoccupied with private pleasures at the expense of public virtue.

The Society of Arts building in the Adelphi, from Adam's Works. *Publication of the building may have been prompted partly by rivalry with Chambers, who had designed the Society's previous Great Room and was about to build the Royal Academy's new premises nearby in Somerset House.*

Doubtless disappointed by George III's patronage to date (and possibly by the loss of the Somerset House commission in 1774 to William Robinson, who died the following year) the brothers end the fourth preface on a provocative and pessimistic note:

> yet we must not expect that the fine arts will ever meet with their most ample reward, or attain their utmost degree of perfection, deprived as they are of that emulation which is excited by public works, and by the honourable applause of a refined and discerning Public.

Sadly, the public buildings included in all three volumes of the *Works* have suffered since Adam's day. The Admiralty screen (1759–61) was altered in 1827, and later restored. The construction of the Register House in Edinburgh, which began in 1774, was supervised by John Adam and the building was still incomplete on Robert's death in 1792. Extensions were soon added by Sir Robert Reid and W. H. Playfair and the open setting has been reduced. For Adam's best-known public building, it is surprisingly traditional in its debts to the British Palladian school.

Edinburgh University falls short of fulfilling Adam's ambition of leaving 'behind me a monument of my talents'. Despite the fact that Adam owed the commission to the University's Principal, William Robertson, his first cousin, construction only commenced in 1789, was continued in 1815 by Reid (with a single, rather than double, court) and in 1834 by Playfair. In 1906 a dome was added by Sir Rowland Anderson to the entrance facade. Nevertheless, seen from the pavement the entrance facade on South Bridge Street is a faithful realization of Adam's design and in the sloping street has a monumentality in its 'movement' that is more sublime than picturesque.

The Royal Society of Arts today appears unchanged from John Street from the engraving published in the *Works*, and provides a striking contrast with Edinburgh University in its elegant surface decoration. Similar in design was the new facade to the Theatre Royal, Drury Lane, commissioned by the architects' friend David Garrick in 1775 (the present building, by Benjamin Wyatt, dates from 1810–12).

The twin towers at Mistley in Essex are all that remains today of the church to which the Adam brothers devoted three plates in the second volume of the *Works*. Even as towers alone these landmarks alongside an estuary confirm Robert Adam's sensitivity to the settings of his buildings and his love of those 'picturesque' effects he so admired in the works of Vanbrugh. But like most of these 'public buildings', it was not a public commission.

There is a note of pathos in the architects' attempt to illustrate this, the highest genre of architecture, from their own works, and it may not be ironic that their examples confirm the nature of British patronage lamented in their preface. Nowhere is this more true than

Edinburgh University, Adam's best-known public building today, was completed in a modified form after his death. (A F Kersting)

St Mary's Church, Mistley, Essex, from the Works. *The larger of only two Adam churches, Mistley was designed from 1776 as part of a commission for Richard Rigby, Paymaster-General of the Forces for his fashionable spa on the banks of the River Stour. Unlike St Andrew's, Gunton, Norfolk (1765–9), only the towers survive.*

in the following, concluding part of volume one.

Designs for the King and Queen

The dedication of the *Spalatro* volume to George III in 1764 and its exhortation to the new king to follow the example of Augustus could have seemed a little embarrassing by the time volume one of the *Works* was completed in 1778. The final part, entitled 'Designs for the King and Queen, and the Princess Dowager of Wales, &c' raises high expectations, particularly as Robert Adam had been appointed, with William Chambers, 'Joint Architect of His Majesty's Works' in 1761, and was succeeded by his brother James in 1768.

Among the eight subjects chosen to illustrate royal patronage not one actual building will be found. Instead of a great urban palace there is 'a Gateway for Carleton House . . . for her Royal Highness the late Princess Dowager of Wales . . . ' together with several details of this design. We are assured 'that she had determined to carry them into execution, if the declining state of her health had not prevented any steps from being taken'. Of the two designs for chimneypieces, one 'is executed in the great saloon of the Queens House' (Buckingham Palace) but the other was only 'proposed for a room in the palace of St James's'. Other works designed for the Queen and reproduced are a painted ceiling for a Japanned Room, a design for a sedan chair and 'an Illumination and Transparency, part of which was executed, by command of the Queen in June 1762, in honour of his Majesty's birth-day'. The latter, a temporary structure dating from six months after Robert Adam's royal appointment, was intended to consist of seventeen paintings on translucent material lit from behind by 400 gas lamps. As Adam says, only 'part' was built, but it failed to inspire commissions from the King. A glance at the design dates on the engravings (ranging from 1762 to 1771) underlines the sense of the brothers searching through old files for material to use.

As usual, the final engraving is devoted to furniture, and once again Robert Adam's versatility as a designer is revealed, this time with a design for a harpsichord 'executed in London for the Empress of Russia'. Alas, this sad parade ends on a familiar refrain with a comment on this last example which concludes the entire volume: 'This design was considerably altered by the person who executed the work.'

The preface to this fifth part struck a more rousing note, asserting the primary status of architecture over the other fine arts. In patriotic contrast to the previous preface, eighteenth-century Britain is compared to sixteenth-century Italy. Britain's turn has come in the 'progress of nations' and the awakening of 'national genius' is seen as a consequence of a widespread improvement in taste:

> The progress of all these arts in Great Britain may be considered as the peculiar distinction of the present reign. Inferior to our ancestors in science, we surpass them in taste. The study of what is elegant and beautiful, sensibility, discernment, and a correctness of eye, are become more general; and arts formerly little known begin to be naturalized amongst us. Cherished by the patronage of a people, opulent, discerning, and capable of estimating merit, the genius of native artists has been called forth into new and laudable exertions.

A sceptical note is sounded about the state and prospects of British painting in order to underline architecture's greater claim to reflect the nation's rise: 'A British school of painting may be gradually formed, and vie for eminence with those of other nations. Architecture has already become more elegant and more interesting.' Unlike painting, British architecture has a native ancestry stretching back through Campbell, Gibbs and Kent via Vanbrugh and Christopher Wren to Inigo Jones, who 'introduced into his country a love of that elegance and refinement which characterise the productions of Greece and Rome'.

The brothers recognize that their principles are now widely shared and claim some credit for their dissemination:

> The parade, the convenience, and social pleasures of life, being better understood, are more strictly attended to in the arrangement and disposition of apartments. Greater variety of form, greater beauty in design, greater gaiety and elegance of ornament, are introduced into interior decoration; while the outside composition is more simple, more grand, more varied in its contour, and imposes on the mind from the superior magnitude and movement of its parts.
>
> Without detracting from the talents and merit of other artists, we are encouraged, by the public approbation, to flatter ourselves, that our works have somewhat contributed to diffuse juster ideas and a better taste in architecture.

The spread of the Adam style is thus far more than the fashionable imitation of a particular family of architects. Their influence is seen as both a cause and consequence of Britain's arrival at its own Renaissance.

Town Houses

Town houses were the Adam brothers' main new projects in the 1770s and three London houses dominate the second volume of the *Works* (published 1776–9). The inclusion of only one preface in the entire second volume suggests that the brothers had more pressing interests than theory. At this time they sought to recover from the risk of bankruptcy over the Adelphi project, just when the outbreak of war in the American colonies made architecture seem an indulgent investment.

The stairwell at Home House, London, designed by Robert Adam in 1775–7.
One of the best examples of 'movement' applied to a town house, it rises the full
height of the building, providing a cylindrical domed lightwell and social axis for
receptions. (Conway Library, Courtauld Institute of Art)

Coming after the climactic discussion of public buildings and national genius that closes the first volume, the town houses and their preface seem incongruous. In the popular appreciation of Adam this century the London town houses have been overshadowed by the celebrated country house commissions, yet in terms of appreciating the authentic Adam style the town houses have an important role. As mentioned above in the discussion of patronage, they provided Robert Adam with the best opportunities in which to display his true genius, and this proved to be the architectural genre in which he was most imitated. Unfortunately most Adam town houses are now corporate headquarters, clubs, private offices, or have been demolished.

The London town houses illustrated are Derby House in Grosvenor Square (1773–4, demolished 1862); Wynn House at

20 St James's Square (1772–4) and Shelburne (later Lansdowne) House in Berkeley Square (c.1762–7, mostly demolished 1930s). Of these only Wynn House survives today (as a company headquarters) but it suffered war damage and has lost its Adam furniture. In fact, the architects' work in the salons of central London is better known through the survival of salvaged rooms in museums. For example, the drawing-room from Lansdowne House has been in the Philadelphia Museum of Art since 1931 and the same house's dining room has been in the Metropolitan Museum, New York since 1932. The Glass Drawing Room from Northumberland House, c.1773–5, and a ceiling from the Adelphi are in the Victoria and Albert Museum. Home House, 20 Portman Square (1775–7), the best

preserved, is familiar to generations of art historians as the first home of the Courtauld Institute of Art.

London houses were not the place for an architect to make public statements to every passer-by. One reason for this was purely practical, as the text accompanying the engraving of the entrance to Wynn House explains: 'It is not a space of forty-six feet, which is the whole extent of the elevation, that an architect can make a great display of talents.' Indoors however, restrictions in space could be readily turned into opportunities by Adam, as a challenge to his love of practical but picturesque planning.

Creating urban palaces from compact terraced houses gave Robert Adam the freedom to plan his reception suites without

The theatrical effect of Adam's interior decoration is epitomized by the engraving in the Works *of the 'Third Drawing-room' at Derby House (1773). The development of the Adam style becomes striking when the sparkling, magical atmosphere of Derby House, with its gilt decoration and satin hangings, is compared with Kenwood's 'great room' of 1764–70 (see page 30). The latter seems, by comparison, quite sober, even sublime.*

always modifying an earlier building. At the same time he had to avoid revealing the property's slender proportions and limited natural light.

In describing recent alterations to Derby House the text to the engraved floor plans (see page 21) explains:

> The smallness of the sites upon which most houses in London are built, obliges the artists of this country to arrange the apartments of the Ladies and Gentlemen on two floors. . . . The French, in their great hotels . , .would introduce both these apartments upon the principal floor.

Despite this fundamental difference,

> both these plans exhibit an attempt to arrange the apartments in the French style, which, as hath been observed in a former part of this work, is best calculated for the convenience and

The Etruscan Room at Osterley Park, London, c.1775–9. Essentially, the Etruscan style consisted of the familiar Adam repertoire of sphinxes, urns, garlands and medallions painted in the colours of red and black figure vases, and set against a blue/green ground. (A.F. Kersting)

elegance of life. . . . the suite of withdrawing-rooms on the principal floor is noble, and well suited to every occasion of public parade.

The plans reveal the ingenious application of the concept of 'movement' as changes in direction and the variety of room shapes create surprise and a greater sense of space.

The spatial adventures of Adam town houses were not unique: as early as 1766, James Paine experimented with a circular toplit staircase, D-shaped rooms and others with apsidal ends in Lord Petre's house in Park Lane. William Kent's staircase and ceiling decorations at 44 Berkeley Square also preceded Adam's town house designs. Taylor, Samuel Wyatt, Soane and Dance (but not Chambers) all sought to employ varied shapes for rooms to escape the ordered predictability of successive rectangles.

Like the general layout of town houses, interior decoration had to be worthy of the opulent lifestyle of competing hostesses, and dazzle their fashionable guests. The 'Adam style' of the 1770s and 80s is particularly suited to confined, candlelit spaces, in its love of intense, linear decoration running over mirrors, through pilasters and lining lunettes like gilded cobwebs. Painted ovals, marbling, *grotesques*, matching carpets and ceilings and other favourites from the Adam repertoire were refined and compressed together, to an exquisite pitch.

Relief from this sense of artistic introversion came from another innovation. The preface to the first part of this second volume opens 'From this Number, persons of taste will, no doubt, observe, that a mode of Decoration has been attempted, which differs from any thing hitherto [p]ractised in Europe'. The first example given of the new mode is the Countess of Derby's dressing-room, its colouring and ornament 'imitated from the vases and urns of the Etruscans'. Robert Adam's fresh inspiration came not as a result of another archaeological expedition but from seeing the collection of earthenware vases excavated by Sir William Hamilton when Ambassador to Naples 'which, having been afterwards purchased by Government, make part of that noble and useful collection of natural and artificial curiosities, which is contained in the British Museum'.

Part of the appeal of the 'Etruscan' vases (the term was used erroneously in the eighteenth century for all Greek and Roman black and red figure pottery) was Adam's conviction that Etruria predated the Greek influence on Rome, and was thus the true source of Roman architecture.

Today, the best example surviving of Adam's 'Etruscan' style is the dressing room at Osterley, where Adam achieves his ambition of unity of style across media, without becoming overwhelming. Adam's 'Etruscan' style underlines his inventive use of sources, and indicates a desire to find an alternative 'Adam style' in an undiscovered source that might trump his rivals.

The first two volumes of the *Works* were published to promote the brothers' practice and to distinguish genuine commissions from 'Adamatic' imitations. Ironically, they encouraged the spread of the style in a debased form. Despite the relatively limited circulation of the luxurious numbers and volumes, they provided architects and builders with a convenient copybook of designs that might be incorporated into their own pattern books. The readiness of the brothers to provide designs for builders of town houses, to supply ornament cast in Adam's patent stucco to rival architects in London, and to use other mass reproduction techniques, contributed to the continuing spread of their influence, albeit in stereotyped, diluted form.

In 1756 Robert Adam wrote of a scheme to publish designs for parks and gardens in a way that almost foretold the fate of the *Works* twenty years later:

But we think it would be vastly imprudent to publish them, as that would be throwing your most precious works into the public's hands. . . . It would enable them to execute without your advice; besides that the best drawing you can imagine, when engraved by Vivares, loses its spirit and appears an ordinary work. They, like Baldy, would cry out; is this all the famous Adam can do? . . . whereas leaving the connoisseurs . . . to judge of and criticise them, your fame spreads in a more polite way and every dirty artist in London has them not to spit at over a mug of porter.

Castles and Villas

The third volume of the *Works*, published in 1822, was not conceived by the Adam brothers. However, a wholly separate publication had been planned by the brothers themselves, which failed to come to fruition. Devoted to castles and villas, particularly of the last years of the brothers' careers, it has recently been reconstructed by Professor Alastair Rowan from finished drawings intended for engraving preserved in Sir John Soane's Museum. Recent research has established the importance of Adam's castles, as evidence both of his achievements and aspirations.

Adam's castles have long been regarded as unscholarly examples of the Georgian 'Gothick' revival, and heirs to Horace Walpole's Strawberry Hill (remodelled from 1752), lacking any authority or sincerity in their apparent cladding of classically proportioned country houses with fancy dress turrets and battlements. In fact, they can be linked directly with Emperor Diocletian's palace and with the brothers' early work in their father's practice. The late villas are no less surprising in their source of inspiration. The castles and villas, together with the rediscovered project for their publication, raise the question once again as to which of their styles and achievements the brothers finally came to value most highly.

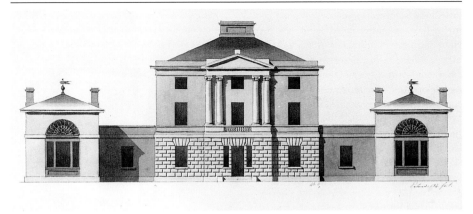

Robert Adam's design for Rosebank House, conceived two months before his death in 1792. The design bears a striking resemblance to Marble Hill House, Twickenham. (By courtesy of the Trustees of Sir John Soane's Museum)

The volume was conceived around 1785 but remained unfinished on the death of James Adam in October 1794. It would have comprised some 47 designs for 36 different castles and villas, of which at least 16 commissions were realized. Unfortunately only three castles are still largely intact today, inside and without (Caldwell, Culzean, Seton) and only one classical villa (Kirkdale) can provide a reliable example of this genre.

Rather than statesmen and leading aristocrats like Lord Bute, Lord Mansfield and the Duke of Northumberland, patrons in these later years were members of the professions, churchmen, merchants and lesser Scottish nobility. Adam worked with renewed intensity after the building recession of the late 1770s, with over 20 Scottish commissions for private houses after 1780 compared to about eight before, over half of which were designed in 1790–92.

Villas were appropriate to men of more finite means, who might not aspire to ancestral seats set within country estates. The quintessential English villa is Marble Hill House, built beside the Thames at Twickenham in 1724–9 by Roger Morris for Henrietta Howard, mistress of George II. Better known is Lord Burlington's Chiswick

House (1726–9), but as a wing to a larger Jacobean family home it lacked the practical self-sufficiency of a villa. Both are indebted to the villas of Palladio, and favour symmetry and mathematical harmony in plan and elevation. However, Adam was not entirely dependent upon the architecture and text books of the Anglo-Palladian tradition, for he had admired Venetian villas at first hand with Clérisseau while sailing by the banks of the Brenta.

Two of Adam's designs for villas seem particularly Palladian. Adam's design for Newliston House, West Lothian (c.1789–91) echoes this tradition and, more directly, Kenwood, London, in the use of a rusticated ground floor and the lack of decorative embellishment. The geometry of the design and cut of the masonry have to stand alone, for there are no applied panels of 'Adam' ornament. Robert Adam's last signed and dated designs are for Rosebank, conceived some two months before his death in 1792. The villa was never built but the design is directly indebted to Marble Hill, probably via the engraving in *Vitruvius Britannicus*. In its avoidance of surface decoration in the 'Adam style', Rosebank contrasts with Robert Adam's own early Palladian designs, such as the library for the Royal College of Physicians in Edinburgh of 1758. Indeed, Robert's late villa designs seem closer to the early sketches of his brother James, whose contribution cannot be underestimated.

The interest in medieval and earlier architecture lying behind the castles included in the unpublished volume is an alternative theme running through the brothers' careers from similarly deep roots. Numerous early sketches survive by Robert and James of Gothic ornament and of neo-Gothic fantasies.

There are some earlier examples of the brothers' work in this genre, particularly Wedderburn Castle, Berwickshire (1770–8) and Mellerstain (c.1770–8). However, the most celebrated examples are Culzean Castle, Strathclyde (1777–92) and Seton Castle near Edinburgh (1789–91), two dramatic conceptions imbued with a rugged spirit. Culzean Castle, the largest example of Adam's work in this genre to be built, was begun in 1777 but the cliff-top north front facing the sea was conceived from 1785 and only completed in 1791. Seton Castle, begun in 1789, was the last work Adam both designed and built, and it remains today one of the least altered of all Adam buildings.

Seen as neo-Gothic, these commissions seem hopelessly inaccurate, their plans and elevations betraying a Georgian love of symmetry. Plans remain axial and outside the accent is more horizontal than vertical. There are no pointed arches, traceried windows, buttresses or pinnacles and Culzean and Seton, for example, can even boast square and round arched Palladian windows among the arrow slits. At Seton Robert Adam went so far as to have a genuine medieval peel-tower demolished and the site cleared before work could commence, reusing materials from the original building.

However, if instead of evaluating such commissions in terms of genuine Gothic buildings they are compared with sources such as Vanbrugh's Castle at Blackheath, Scottish castles (including those constructed by William Adam and his sons), the ducal palaces of Renaissance Italy, and sixteenth-century French châteaux with their round towers and battlements, Adam's castles take on a different meaning. Adam's artistic interests can be seen to extend beyond any inability to escape the Georgian commitment to symmetry to a powerful response to less conventional architectural sources and to the unique settings offered in Scotland. Adam's response makes ornament take second place to form, to the sculptural composition of mass and volume, and to a Picturesque landscape painter's sensitivity to sunlight and shadow.

The attraction and importance of the castles to Robert Adam become clear in the light of the ambitions expressed in the *Spalatro* volume, and in the *Works*. As an artist, seeking inspiration from the complete setting of his buildings, Robert Adam would have found the open Scottish landscapes ideal as locations for grand statements. To an intellectual, aspiring to design public

At Culzean Castle, Strathclyde, Robert Adam incorporated an oval staircase well (1787) into the middle of an earlier castle. (A.F. Kersting)

buildings, castles offered the necessary scale through which an architect might address the public 'mind'. As an architect of endless versatility, he had sought to overcome the absence of truly major commissions by integrating the scale and spirit of public works into domestic architecture, as in his designs for the facades of Luton Hoo and Kedleston. However, Scottish castles provided opportunities to compose on a colossal, even sublime, scale with fewer limitations set by remodelling earlier buildings, as occurred in his English country houses. Unfortunately, the end result might have to overrule some of the needs of comfortable living. For example, in Adam's unexecuted designs for Barnbougle Castle, the Earl of Rosebery's bedroom was to measure 35 by 16 feet, while his valet was to enjoy a rotunda 16 feet in diameter.

Adam was also a Scot, of course, and it is tempting to speculate whether any patriotic or stronger political spirit lay behind his readiness to build for Scottish barons palaces

on a scale he had sought to build for the Hanoverian English King. In the dedication to the *Spalatro* volume Adam had sought to inspire George III to commission something comparable to Emperor Diocletian's great fortified palace. Twenty or more years later, his ambition unfulfilled, Robert Adam turned his energies back to the 'North Britons' whose countrymen had helped to launch his career. Whereas his father had built a string of forts after the 1745 rebellion to act as a modern Hadrian's Wall, Robert Adam now designed a series of palaces where reclusive Scots might choose to emulate Diocletian.

One clue that could provide some confirmation of this speculation over the ideas behind Adam's castles is an unpublished essay written shortly after Robert Adam's death by John Clerk of Eldin, Robert's brother in law, with whom the architect stayed every summer during his annual visits to Edinburgh in the 1780s.

Robert Adam's design for the north elevation of Culzean Castle, 1785. (By courtesy of the Trustees of Sir John Soane's Museum)

The north front of Culzean Castle today, rising impressively from rocky cliffs above the Irish Sea. (A.F. Kersting)

Clerk believed Gothic to have been 'peculiarly dedicated to religious purposes', whereas the best source for castles, he believed, was Anglo-Saxon and Norman (otherwise known as Romanesque) architecture. He traced the Romanesque tradition through to Elizabethan palaces and houses, a tradition which he saw as the inspiration for Adam's later castle style.

Baronial castles were valued by Clerk (and in turn, we may assume, by Adam) as the direct descendants of the buildings of the Roman conquest, and hence, of Roman Imperial architecture. Behind this alternative tradition lay the reconciliation of those seeming opposites, Gothic and classical architecture, a reunion Adam may have sought since his first arrival in Italy.

Some interesting parallels exist between Adam's reconstruction of the defensive outer walls of Diocletian's palace and his last castle, Seton. There is, for example, the preference for a solid parapet instead of battlements, the symmetrical arrangement of rounded windows and the even, balanced spacing of towers. Even the so-called 'Diocletian window' (a recessed semi-circle derived from Adam's study of the public baths of Rome) features in Adam's designs for Culzean and Seton.

Rather than half-heartedly adding a Scottish baronial flavour to Georgian neoclassical architecture, Robert Adam turned to his records of over twenty years before for inspiration. The result was a style of architecture that could claim direct descent from Roman architects, by-passing the Palladian tradition, and making 'Bob the Roman' their true heir.

Decline and Fall

Critics and Competition

This study has introduced the architecture of Robert Adam in terms of the buildings he preferred, and in terms of the architectural theories he shared with his brother James. Such a study cannot conclude without considering how others saw the Adam brothers, their buildings and writings, especially in their own lifetimes.

Robert and James Adam may have laid great stress on public buildings, and found some fulfilment in Scottish castles, but it was the surface decoration, characteristic of the 'Adam style' of the 1770s, with which they were most identified by their contemporaries. Critics favoured analogies with food – pastry, cheesecake, gingerbread – and with the dressing room, as if the 'Adam style' was indulgent, insubstantial, superficially attractive, and the product of passing fashion. Rival architects spoke out, finding the tone of the *Works* offensive in its pretentious claims to have made innovations others might regard as their own, whilst one of its central themes, the creative freedom of the architect to break away from Palladian rules, was regarded by some as anarchy.

A rational analysis, which helped to seal the brothers' unpopularity in the nineteenth century, pointed to the origins of the 'Adam style' in the ruins of the Emperor Diocletian's palace, as if late Roman Imperial architecture was degenerate and the brothers were essentially stylistic revivalists, starting from a false premiss. Unfortunately, this limited understanding of the principles and aspirations behind the brothers' buildings continued even when the 'Adams' revival began in earnest from 1867, and produced a Victorian fashion for furniture and interior decoration based on their repertoire of ornament. In the twentieth century popular understanding of Adam architecture still centres on the 'Adam style' of interior decoration, particularly in country houses open to the public. Just as the *Works* challenged the over-familiar Palladian perception of classical architecture, so today there is an established view of Adam architecture, which is, however, beginning to be undermined in favour of designs, buildings and ideas that have previously been left in the wings.

Opposition to the brothers in their own lifetimes was not provoked by their success, style of architecture or the arrogant claims of the *Works* alone. A turning point (which coincided with the publication of the first part of the *Works*) was the financial collapse of the Adelphi project. The Adelphi (its name taken from the Greek αδελφοι, meaning brothers) included terraced streets modestly entitled Robert, John and Adam Street behind 'Royal Terrace'. The financial collapse of this vast speculative venture was avoided by a lottery in 1774, but the ambitious enterprise revealed the brothers as victims of their own hubris, like characters in a Greek tragedy. The idea of raising a great terrace fronting the Thames was compared at the time to the marine wall and terraces of Diocletian's palace facing the Adriatic, only here the palace was for wealthy professionals and the more fashionable upper middle classes. Such pretensions, together with the external application of the Adam style of ornament, could not fail to prompt criticism. Enemies had been made, particularly the leaders of the City of London who had petitioned the King not to grant royal assent to the development. The public failure meant not only a loss of business, but of confidence among the brothers' admirers.

Horace Walpole is the most quoted of Adam's critics; indeed, he created an enduring vocabulary for describing the 'Adam style'. Walpole had been an early admirer of Robert Adam. In the preface to his *Anecdotes of Painting* (1761) he had written 'Architecture …seems reviving. The taste and skill of Mr Adam is formed for public works.' In June 1773 Walpole had praised Osterley following the first phase of Adam's remodelling, as 'oh! the palace of palaces' where the Drawing Room seemed 'worthy of Eve before the Fall'.

Walpole's change of heart occurred at the time of the Adelphi fiasco and seems also to have been prompted by reading the first preface to the *Works*, with its claim that the Adam style had been 'servilely copied or misapplied'. Walpole took the preface to be written by Robert alone, and in 1773 wrote to a friend defending James Wyatt, to whom he believed Adam must be alluding in this accusation of plagiarism. (Wyatt himself later admitted 'that when he came from Italy he found the public taste so corrupted by the

The Antechamber, or Tapestry Room, at Osterley Park House, c.1775. is hung with Gobelins tapestries representing the Elements. Horace Walpole described the room as 'enriched by Adam in his best taste, except that he has stuck diminutive heads in bronze, no bigger than a half-crown, into the chimney-piece's hair'. (A.F. Kersting)

A detail from the ceiling of the Long Gallery at Harewood House, Yorkshire, c.1768–9. It was work of this kind that Chambers probably had in mind when criticising Adam's 'trifling gaudy ceilings'. Robert Adam had succeeded the Yorkshire architect John Carr at Harewood, and much of his interior decoration still remains. (A.F. Kersting)

Adams and he was obliged to comply with it'.) In the same letter Walpole described the entrance screen at Syon House as 'all lace and embroidery'. The Adelphi buildings, with their light-industrial basements surmounted by elegantly decorated terraces, are 'Warehouses, laced down the seam, like a soldier's trull in a regimental old coat'.

A return visit to Osterley in 1778 provided Walpole with a further opportunity to exercise his bitter wit, for in the interim the Antechamber (Tapestry Room), State Bedroom and Etruscan Room had been completed, the last in the more extreme linear style which still divides his admirers today. In particular, Walpole disliked the state bed (conceived by Adam as a temple to Venus) which seemed 'like a modern head-dress, for round the outside of the dome are festoons of artificial flowers. What would Vitruvius think of a dome decorated by a milliner?' The next room, in Adam's 'Etruscan' style, seemed 'a profound tumble into the Bathos. It is going out of a palace into a potter's field.'

Walpole's best-known criticisms, which serve so well to evoke the later Adam style of interior decoration, were made after admiring the work of rival architects. For example, in 1782 he described Portman House, built by 'Athenian' Stuart in Portman Square for Elizabeth Montagu, as 'grand, not tawdry, nor larded and embroidered and pomponned with shreds and remnants and *cliquant* like all the harlequinades of Adam, which never let the eye repose a moment'. No doubt Walpole had in mind Home House, also in Portman Square, where Adam had created his most extreme interiors for a rival hostess. Three years later, after admiring Henry Holland's work at Carlton House, Walpole delivered his most haunting sentence: 'How sick one shall be after this chaste palace, of Mr Adam's gingerbread and sippets of embroidery.'

Like Walpole, William Chambers took exception to the first preface to the *Works*, but he considered the accusation of plagiarism to be personal. He protested to Lord Grantham about 'a preface, rather presumptuous, as I am told for I have not yet read the book' in which the Adam brothers 'boast of having first brought the true Style of Decoration into England and that all the architects of the present day are only servile copyers of their excellence'. In his defence, Chambers cited his latest work 'Melbourne House, decorated in a manner almost diametrically opposite to theirs; and more, as I flatter myself, in the true style, as approaching nearer to the most approved style of the Ancients'.

Chambers's retort is another reminder that the brothers' claims to be innovators should not be believed at face value, despite the fact that they have come down through history largely unchallenged. At the same time, competing architects cannot be expected to praise one another's work. Adam believed that his path to royal patronage was blocked by Chambers, and his rival's position as Treasurer to the Royal Academy must account for his absence from the ranks of Academicians.

Chambers did not stop at defending his own work from association with the Adam style and at claiming its greater affinity with classical architecture. He spoke out against the 'filigree toy work' of the style and (presumably with the red drawing-room at Syon in mind) criticised 'the trifling gaudy ceilings, now in fashion, which, composed as they are of little rounds, squares, hexagons, and ovals, excite no other idea than that of a dessert upon the plates of which are dished out bad copies of indifferent antiques'.

Another rival architect, James Paine, criticised the brothers for this seemingly unintelligible use of detail, shortly after they had taken his place at Kedleston. In the first volume of his *Plans, Elevations and Sections of Noblemen and Gentlemen's Houses* (1767) Paine sounded a warning against the sacrifice of 'convenience and propriety to the modes of the most despicable ruins of ancient Greece. ...let them continue to give the forms of triumphal arches, to the fronts of dwelling houses, and to copy the mouldings and

ornaments of the ancients, upon so small a scale, that the parts may not be discerned at the distance of the height of a common room'. Recent research on Paine has revealed the Palladian architect's own interest in 'movement' and in house planning, and his preference for the villa with wings over the seventeenth-century 'house of parade'.

The best summary of contemporary criticism of the Adam style of architecture is contained within a vitriolic pamphlet written in 1779 by the painter Robert Smirke and Wyatt's assistant William Porden. At that time Smirke painted decorative panels for Wyatt's interiors. Essentially, Smirke and Porden criticised the lack of coherent principles to replace the rules of the classical tradition, which the Adams seemed to reject entirely in favour of artistic genius. 'Genius' they declared 'is a happy madness that decides and determines without thought, reflection or foresight. Such is the genius of the Adams. ... Their works are not only erected without Rules, but from them no Rules can be drawn.' Secondly, they could not accept the employment of the Adam style of decoration for the exteriors of buildings. They gave credit to 'Athenian' Stuart for questioning the use of external architectural features indoors

The south, garden front of Kedleston Hall, Derbyshire (c.1760–68). Adam's allusion to a Roman triumphal arch in the design was criticised by his rival James Paine, whom he succeeded at Kedleston. (A.F. Kersting)

The south front of Kenwood, London, 1773, showing the refined linear style of exterior ornament which Adam pioneered, and others soon criticised.

by architects of the Palladian school, and accused Adam of committing the same offence only in reverse, in using domestic scale ornament on his facades:

> Most of the white walls, with which Mr Adam has speckled this city, are no better than Models for the Twelfth-Night-Decoration of a Pastry Cook.

Early in the nineteenth century, John Soane's Royal Academy lectures (delivered between 1810 and 1837) offered a view of the Adam style which has continued well into the this century. He described 'a light and fanciful style of decoration, better suited for private buildings...ill-suited to external grandeur: the Messrs. Adam had not formed their taste on the best examples of antiquity...'. Such a criticism cannot be made of the Adam

buildings of the 1760s, the public buildings of Edinburgh, or the villas and Scottish castles; Soane must have had in mind the surface ornament used along the terraces of the Adelphi, the south front of Kenwood and the 'Adamatic' buildings from which the brothers wished to dissociate themselves through publishing their genuine *Works*.

The idea that the brothers' careers had been ill founded on a poor example of late Roman imperial architecture became doctrine through its inclusion in an influential *Encyclopaedia of Architecture* by Joseph Gwilt, published in 1842 when the Adam brothers' reputation reached its nadir. Gwilt regretted that 'the ornaments of Diocletian's Palace at Spalatro, should have loaded our dwellings... the depraved compositions of Adam were... the works of a man who was content to draw his supplies from so vitiated a source'. The 'Adams revival' of the late Victorian era did little to dispel this view, drawing as it did on the designs of the 1770s to inspire the furnishing of elegant interiors rather than reappraising the brothers' general architectural achievement. As late as 1922, when he published his two-volume study of Robert and James Adam, A.T. Bolton lamented that Smirke's pamphlet was still echoed in 'those current prejudices which it is the object of this work to dispel'.

Conclusion

Two hundred years after the death of Robert Adam, the popular image of Britain's best-known architect is still too tightly framed. The demolition of most of the Adelphi in 1936, together with the destruction of many of London's 'Adamatic' terrace houses, has helped to dislodge the overworn criticism that his exterior architectural ornament belonged in the boudoir. But in its place a public perception of Adam as a designer first and foremost of grand domestic interiors has become established, thanks to the creation of Adam 'period rooms' in museums since the 1930s and the increasing accessibility of country houses, particularly since the 1950s.

More recently, the practical use of such rooms, and the ideas they were intended to convey to their erudite visitors, have been recognized as determining factors in every detail of the brothers' designs; the castles and villas have emerged with an increasing status and for the first time a complete survey of buildings and sculptural monuments has been published (see Further Reading).

However, for one of Britain's greatest artists, Robert Adam himself remains remarkably unknown. The extent to which his claims to be an architectural innovator are justified still needs to be established in print; his political interests remain unresearched, while the economics of the vast family firm, William Adam and Co., need to be unravelled if the full variety of business pressures are to be recognized among the architect's motivations. The patrons of the various architectural genre, their social or political affiliations and how they compared with the patrons of Adam's rivals, are further questions beyond the scope of this book.

The mind of Robert Adam, as an architectural theorist, may never be extracted from the writings of his brother James, but the ideas briefly discussed in this book link directly into the wider debates of the era, and these issues are receiving increasing attention today. Fortunately, even if Robert Adam himself remains tantalizingly elusive, there is no doubt that we can still recognize and enjoy (to quote Sir John Soane once more) 'the *electric power* of this Revolution in Art'.

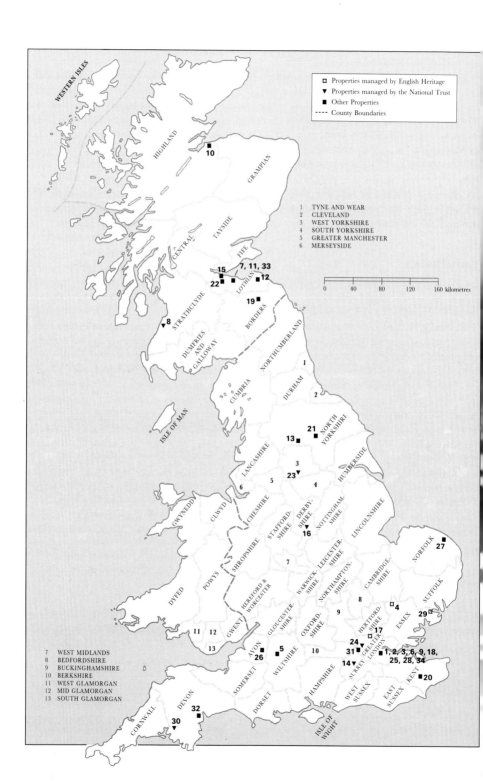

WESTERN ISLES

HIGHLAND

GRAMPIAN

TAYSIDE

FIFE

CENTRAL

STRATHCLYDE

LOTHIAN

BORDERS

DUMFRIES AND GALLOWAY

NORTHUMBERLAND

ISLE OF MAN

CUMBRIA

DURHAM

NORTH YORKSHIRE

LANCASHIRE

HUMBERSIDE

GWYNEDD

CLWYD

CHESHIRE

STAFFORD-SHIRE

DERBY-SHIRE

NOTTINGHAM-SHIRE

LINCOLNSHIRE

NORFOLK

DYFED

POWYS

SHROPSHIRE

HEREFORD & WORCESTER

GLOUCESTER-SHIRE

WARWICK-SHIRE

LEICESTER-SHIRE

NORTHAMPTON-SHIRE

CAMBRIDGE-SHIRE

SUFFOLK

GWENT

AVON

WILTSHIRE

OXFORD-SHIRE

BEDFORDSHIRE

BUCKINGHAMSHIRE

HERTFORD-SHIRE

ESSEX

SOMERSET

HAMPSHIRE

SURREY

GREATER LONDON

KENT

CORNWALL

DEVON

DORSET

WEST SUSSEX

EAST SUSSEX

ISLE OF WIGHT

⊞ Properties managed by English Heritage
▼ Properties managed by the National Trust
■ Other Properties
---- County Boundaries

1 TYNE AND WEAR
2 CLEVELAND
3 WEST YORKSHIRE
4 SOUTH YORKSHIRE
5 GREATER MANCHESTER
6 MERSEYSIDE

7   WEST MIDLANDS
8   BEDFORDSHIRE
9   BUCKINGHAMSHIRE
10 BERKSHIRE
11 WEST GLAMORGAN
12 MID GLAMORGAN
13 SOUTH GLAMORGAN

0   40   80   120   160 kilometres

10

15
22
7, 11, 33
12
19
8

1
2

21
13

3
23

5

6

4

16

7

8
9

4
29

17
24
31
14

1, 2, 3, 6, 9, 18, 25, 28, 34

20

26
5

32
30

27

Gazetteer: The Major Works of Robert Adam

The map and key indicate selected examples of Adam's work accessible to the public at the time of writing. For a comprehensive list of over 150 buildings, interiors and monuments, including some thought not to be by Adam, see David King, *The Complete Works of Robert Adam* (1991).

1. **Adelphi**, London, 1768–75; demolished 1936; 9 houses survive, plus Society of Arts, John Adam Street, 1771–4.

2. **Admiralty Screen**, Whitehall, London, 1759–61.

3. **Apsley House**, Piccadilly, London, 1771–5.

4. **Audley End**, Essex, 1763–5.

A detail of the magnificent ceiling of the Little Drawing Room, Audley End, Essex, where Robert Adam redecorated the principal living rooms.

5. **Bowood House**, Wiltshire, 1761–71; mausoleum, 1763 (main house demolished).

6. **Chandos House,** 2 Queen Anne Street, London, 1770–71.

7. **Charlotte Square**, Edinburgh, 1791–4.

8. **Culzean Castle**, Strathclyde, 1777–90.

9. **Fitzroy Square**, London, 1790–94 (south and east sides).

10. **Fort George**, Highland, 1748–69.

11. **General Register House**, Edinburgh, 1771–92.

12. **Gosford House**, Lothian, 1790–92.

13. **Harewood House**, North Yorkshire, 1765–9.

14. **Hatchlands Park**, Surrey, 1759.

15. **Hopetoun House**, Lothian, 1750–57.

16. **Kedleston Hall**, Derbyshire, c.1760–68.

17. **Kenwood**, Hampstead, London, 1764–79.

18. **Mansfield Street**, London, 1770–72.

19. **Mellerstain**, Borders, c.1770–8.

20. **Mersham le Hatch**, Kent, 1762–6.

21. **Newby Hall**, North Yorkshire, 1767–76.

22. **Newliston House**, Lothian, c.1789–91.

23. **Nostell Priory**, Wakefield, West Yorkshire, 1766–80.

24. **Osterley Park House**, Osterley, London, 1761–80.

25. **20 Portman Square**, London (Home House), c.1774–6.

26. **Pulteney Bridge**, Bath, Avon, 1768–74.

27. **St Andrew's Church**, Gunton, Norfolk, 1765–9.

28. **20 St James's Square**, London, 1771–4.

29. **St Mary's Church**, Mistley, Essex, 1776 (towers only survive).

The Saloon at Saltram House, Devon, designed by Robert Adam in 1768. Adam also designed the Dining Room. (National Trust Photographic Library/Rob Matheson)

30. **Saltram House**, Devon, 1768–9.

31. **Syon House**, Brentford, London, 1761–9; entrance screen, 1773.

32. **Ugbrooke House**, Devon, 1763–8.

33. **University**, Edinburgh, 1785–93.

34. **Westminster Abbey**, London: **monuments** to Major John Andre (d.1780); Mary Hope (d.1767); Elizabeth, Duchess of Northumberland (d.1776); James Thomson (d.1748); Lt-Col Roger Townshend (d.1759); William Dalrymple (d.1782).

Selected Sources and Further Reading

Adam, Robert, *Ruins of the Palace of the Emperor Diocletian, at Spalatro in Dalmatia* (London 1764).

Adam, Robert and Adam, James *The Works in Architecture of Robert and James Adam* (London, 1773-1822).

Beard, Geoffrey *The Works of Robert Adam* (Edinburgh, 1978).

Bolton, A.T. *The Architecture of Robert and James Adam* (London, 1922).

Fleming, John *Robert Adam and his Circle in Edinburgh and Rome* (London, 1962).

Harris, John *Sir William Chambers* (London, 1970).

King, David *The Complete Works of Robert and James Adam* (Oxford, 1991).

Leach, Peter *James Paine* (London, 1988).

Lees-Milne, James *The Age of Adam* (London, 1947).

Oresco, Robert (ed.) *The Works in Architecture of Robert and James Adam* (London, 1975).

Rowan, Alastair *Designs for Castles and Country Villas by Robert and James Adam* (Oxford, 1985).

Catalogues of Architectural Drawings in the Victoria and Albert Museum: Robert Adam (London, 1988).

Stillman, Damie *The Decorative Work of Robert Adam* (London, 1973).

Stillman, Damie *English Neo-classical Architecture* (London, 1988).

Summerson, John *Architecture in Britain: 1530 to 1830* (London, 1970).

Sykes, Christopher Simon *Private Palaces. Life in the Great London Houses* (London, 1985).

Yarwood, Doreen *Robert Adam* (London, 1970).